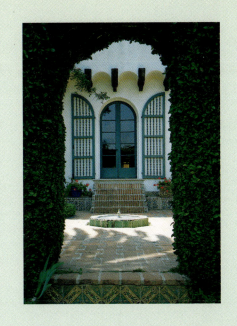

THE

GARDENS

OF

CALIFORNIA

ART CENTER COLLEGE OF DESIGN

THE

GARDENS

OF

CALIFORNIA

**Four Centuries of Design from
Mission to Modern**

Nancy Goslee Power

WITH SUSAN HEEGER

Photographs by Mick Hales

DESIGN BY KC WITHERELL

CLARKSON POTTER/PUBLISHERS
NEW YORK

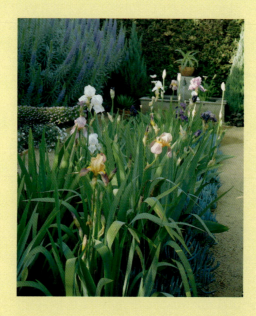

Published by Clarkson N. Potter, Inc., 201 East 50th Street, New
York, New York 10022. Member of the Crown Publishing Group.

Random House, Inc. New York, Toronto, London, Sydney, Auckland.

CLARKSON N. POTTER, POTTER, and colophon
are trademarks of Clarkson N. Potter, Inc.

MANUFACTURED IN CHINA

LIBRARY OF CONGRESS CATALOGING-IN-PUBLICATION DATA
Power, Nancy Goslee.
the gardens of California/by Nancy Goslee Power; photographs by
Mick Hales.—1st ed.
p. cm.
Includes index
1. Gardens—California. 2. Gardens—California—Pictorial works.
I.Title.
SB466.U65C273 1995
712'.09794—dc20 93-43789
CIP
ISBN 0-517-58381-X
10 9 8 7 6 5 4 3 2 1
FIRST EDITION

ACKNOWLEDGMENTS

TO DEREK, for his advice on English spelling versus American, and his encouragement, tolerance, and amazing support.

TO ALL MY FAMILY, AND OLIVER, MY SON, who put up with my absences.

TO MY MOTHER, ELLEN GOSLEE, who passed on to me her passion for gardening and her discerning eye.

TO BUNNY WILLIAMS, for being the friend who was always there for me.

TO HELEN PRATT, "the mother of the project," without whom there would have been no book; she kept it together despite unbelievable obstacles.

TO PHILIP CHANDLER, "You can do it, you know more than you think you do!" A master teacher and mentor.

TO SUSAN HEEGER, who had the patience to listen to me week after week as we wrote the book; her sensitivity to the project and her love of gardens are evident here.

TO SALLY PAUL, my long-term assistant, who reads both my writing and my mind, and to all who have worked with me in my design studio, especially Myva Newman.

TO KATHERINE WHITESIDE, who tightened up the manuscript with her sharp mind and Southern wit!

TO KC WITHERELL, the designer of the book, whose strong, bold, and elegant taste made my dreams come true.

TO ANNETTA HANNA, my editor at Clarkson Potter, whose tenacity as the final editor kept us all on track with great understanding.

TO PEGGY KENNEDY and all my friends at *House Beautiful* who have encouraged me for eighteen years in the field of design.

TO WADE GRAHAM, my kindred spirit, whose irreverent attitude, intelligence, perseverance, and incitement got the book finished while making me laugh.

TO NIKI EKSTROM, whose wisdom and wicked humor kept me in line.

THANK-YOU to all of the garden owners who generously opened their gardens to me.

THANK-YOU also to the following friends, fellow designers, and people who helped: Katherine and Stewart Abercrombie; Valerie Arelt; Mrs. John Bacon; Virginia Baker; Randy Baldwin; Ruth Bancroft; Joan B. Banning; Michael Barclay; George Bass; Sydney Baumgartner; Tina Beebe; Ruth M. Borun; Jamie Bowles; Michael Brown; Tom Buckley; Jack Chandler; Kathleen and Bill Collins; Thomas Cordell; Thomas B. Cox; Peggy and Kellam de Forest; Harriet Doer; Marcia Donahue; Tony Duquette; Gep Durenberger; Garrett Eckbo; Mary Emmerling; Robert Fletcher; Wendy Foster; Frank O. Gehry; Maureen F. Gordon; Susan Gordon; Isabelle Green; Alison Greenberg; John Greenlee; Carol Greentree; Mrs. Richard S. Hambleton; Ed Hardy; Joan Hochaday; Ann James; Anne Jones; Dr. Austin; Ted Kipping; Enid Koffler; Del Kolve; Judy Long; Arturo Lopez; Ann Lounsburg; Lillian and Jon Lovelace; Larry Macpherson; Penny Marsden; Dick Martin; Lynda Martin; Sally McBride; Kacey and Peter McCoy; Jackie and Skip Morgen; David Morton; Mercedes Muirhead; Peter Newton; Cynthia Nolen; Mary Weber Novak; Nancy Novogrod; Victoria Pearson; Johnathan Plant; Gloria Portillo; Suzanne Rhinestein; Christine Rosmini; Donna and Joe Roth; Marna and Rockwell D. Schnabel; Bob Smaus; Martha Stewart; Susan Stringfellow; Bill Strom; Geraldine Stutz; Kate and Andy Summers; Stephen Suzman; Rose Tarlow; Angie Theriot; Brian Tichenor; Alta Tingle; Patsy Tisch; Janet and John Trefethen; Bernardo Urquieta; Carol Valentine; John Vaughn; George Waters; Hutton Wilkinson; Sally Winslow; Paul Wiseman; Jim Yoch; and Buzz Yudell.

contents
preface xii   introduction 2

the california garden
SPANISH BEGINNINGS AND INFLUENCE

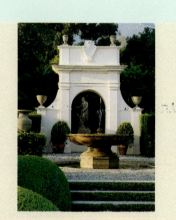

the classic garden
THE GOLDEN AGE OF ESTATE GARDENS

the wild garden
NATURALISM IN DESIGN

CALIFORNIA IS A PARADISE ON THE PACIFIC, a place of mythic proportions blessed with an intoxicating climate. Its monumental natural landscapes, including ocean, mountains, and barren sweeps of desert, fill the senses and invite romantic interpretation. California's wild, idyllic settings have always influenced the development of its man-made landscapes.

All through history human beings have been making gardens that reflect their own images of paradise, and along the way they've discovered better ways of using, sharing, and appreciating their landscape. As a garden designer, I have great interest in the lessons of the past, and I'm constantly aware—as designers must be—of important historical precedents. But like many others in my profession, I have been frustrated by the lack of literature that might provide a design-oriented overview of California's landscape traditions and contribute to an understanding of contemporary style. In a sense, I've written this book because I got tired of waiting for it to appear.

Though I don't claim to have put together the definitive volume on anything—California is too vast and complex a place to be summed up in a single pass—I hope this book will be useful to professionals, garden-loving amateurs, and people who just like to dream about gardens. I want it to be a fantasy book as well as a reference guide, a reflection of the eclectic paradise that is California, full of so many people from so many different places, and noisy with ideas and perspectives. If I can capture the drama of this always emerging landscape, if I can show the influences of its multiple cultures and almost unlimited plant choices, I'll feel I've done a job that needed doing.

The landscapes chosen for this book, whether private or public, all have the one quality that makes great gardens so satisfying: they offer something to inspire the visitor. They give us lessons about appropriate plants and designs, not only for a western context but for broader applications, too. They present interesting distillations of historic garden traditions or, in some cases, they invent their own.

In choosing these private Edens, I have followed my heart as well as my knowledge and professional instincts about seminal California landscape. For example, I've been haunted for years by the intelligence and subtlety of landscape designer Lockwood de Forest's own Santa Barbara garden. Every space outside the windows of his home—which resembles a small-scale Roman villa—is a habitable garden room, and the overall landscape is beautifully sited, incorporating the majesty of distant mountains. There are a few gardens included here simply for their mad exuberance. Ganna Walska's Lotusland in Montecito with its Hollywood theatrics and unearthly plants is one of these, as is Peter Newton's creation outside St. Helena in Northern California. A lush, exotic combination of English and Asian influences, Newton's garden is designed solely for effect, and stands as one man's private vision of nirvana. Phil Chandler's vest-pocket garden around his apartment building in Santa Monica is another one that I have loved for its powerful visual messages: within a small space, it is possible to achieve absolute magic with the right plants and color palette.

Creating a landscape is a highly personal endeavor. While it may involve many different people, it inevitably expresses something heartfelt about our connection to a place. In the vast and diverse territory of California, this expression has taken many forms. But if there is one aspect linking all our gardens here, perhaps it is an appreciation of the majesty of our surroundings, and a desire to get outside and live our lives in the sunshine, under the benevolent skies.

INTRODUCTION

THE FIRST CALIFORNIA GARDENS WERE LAID OUT by Spanish padres around twenty-one missions they built in the late 1700s and early 1800s. Extending from San Diego to Sonoma, the missions—self-contained agricultural centers set in vast tracts of undeveloped land—were meant to solidify Spain's claim to Alta California, while the missionaries befriended and converted the local Native Americans.

Despite their largely utilitarian character (the missionaries grew oranges and other fruit as well as wine grapes and food crops), the design of mission gardens offered the beginnings of an appropriate California model. Based on the gardens of Andalusia in southern Spain, the mission gardens featured walled vineyards and orchards, and enclosed patios with fountains. Some of the mission courtyards also contained axial paths, olive and pepper trees for shade, and simple vegetable and flower beds.

After the missions were secularized in 1822, subsequent settlers—many of them Mexican or Spanish soldiers or land-grant families—built Moorish-style homes and courtyard gardens. These were enclosed on three sides by the walls of the house, with a cool, intimate patio extending the indoor living space and creating a protected area for food cultivation. When American frontiersmen and pioneers arrived in the 1830s and 1840s, they adopted the simple Spanish model for living. Although water for ornamental plants was limited, especially in Southern California, a few East Coast flowers and shrubs were added to those the missionaries had brought from Mexico.

In 1846, California became part of the United States, and gold fever swept great numbers of prospectors and speculators to the West. Overnight, San Francisco became a sophisticated metropolis

THE SIMPLE LINES AND PLANTINGS AT MISSION LA PURÍSIMA CONCEPCIÓN
WERE INITIATED AS EARLY AS 1787, YET REMAIN APPROPRIATE INSPIRATION FOR MODERN CALIFORNIA GARDENS.

AT WILLIAM BOURN'S FILOLI, ELEGANT FORMAL PLANTINGS
CONTRAST WITH THE UNDULATING PROFILE OF THE MOUNTAINS BEYOND.

and, on the peninsula below the city, local tycoons began to build huge estates with lavish gardens.

In 1869, the first transcontinental railway was completed to San Francisco; in 1876 and 1885, the Southern Pacific and then the Santa Fe came to Los Angeles. Romantic novels and travel guides touted the glories and health benefits of California, and newcomers arrived by the thousands. The population of Los Angeles quintupled during the booming 1880s, growing from a sleepy farm center into a city of 50,000 people.

Some who came to Southern California were wealthy eastern and midwestern industrialists wish-ing to retire or to spend their winters in more congenial surroundings than the congested, polluted centers of New York and Chicago. Many settled in Santa Barbara and Pasadena, where especially pleasant climates complemented their Edenic settings.

These arrivals built homes like those they had left and their showy front gardens took traditional American shapes. As with other gardens of that period, they were heavily influenced by the naturalistic, English landscape school as well as by the stylized hodgepodge of the Victorians. Imposing a model they knew on a place they didn't understand, these settlers planted endless sweeps of lawn punctu-

CALIFORNIANS HAVE ALWAYS REVELED IN THE HORTICULTURAL POSSIBILITIES OF THEIR
MEDITERRANEAN CLIMATE. ABOVE: WESTERN HILLS NURSERY. OPPOSITE: THE BANCROFT GARDEN.

ated by hedges, masses of flowers in brilliant colors, and a dizzying jumble of pines, palms, and eucalyptus. As were their former gardens in the inclement East, the new ones were primarily for display; their owners hadn't yet learned how to "live" in them.

About this same time, knowledgeable, cosmopolitan plant collectors, botanists, and nurserymen arrived in California and found a wealth of native flora alongside the Mediterranean plants previously introduced by the Spanish. They also saw that exotics from Australia, South America, South Africa, and similar climates around the world would thrive in the mild conditions of the Golden State.

In 1867, Joseph Sexton opened the first nursery in Santa Barbara, and gained a national reputation for his collection of exotic and tropical plants. Over the next three decades, Kinton Stevens, Charles A. Reed, and John Spence followed suit and opened nurseries, while eminent Italian horticulturist Dr. Francescho Franceschi founded the Southern California Acclimatizing Association to introduce and test new plants suitable for the region. Prominent nurserymen in Los Angeles included Louis Stengel, Jacob Dieterich, and Eugene Germain. Kate Sessions played a parallel and very influential role in San Diego, as did Byron O. Clark in Pasadena. Elsewhere in the state, Englishman Theodore Payne propagated and publicized California's native plants while Luther Burbank experimented in Santa Rosa with a dizzying number of local and imported ornamental and edible hybrids.

Interest in plants and plant collecting approached near-religious zeal during the last years of the nineteenth century. Men like millionaire silver

JOAN BANNING HAS CREATED A WONDERFULLY FLORIFEROUS COTTAGE GARDEN
TO COMPLEMENT HER CALIFORNIA CRAFTSMAN HOUSE IN PASADENA.

magnate Adolph Sutro of San Francisco created vast gardens of flora gathered from far-flung corners of the earth. Sutro Heights, his twenty-one–acre Victorian extravaganza, featured an eclectic collection of trees, flowers, and statuary, complete with a rambling glass conservatory and a garden bed that spelled out his name in lavish blooms.

As the new century dawned, however, the overkill of Victorian taste began to give way to other currents. One of these was the arts and crafts movement born in England in reaction to the hypermechanized world of the Industrial Revolution. California, with its physical beauty and open-minded populace of transplants and pioneers, was fertile ground for a philosophy that celebrated nature and the creative spirit.

These ideas found expression in the clean har-

monies of Craftsman furniture as well as in the architecture of California bungalows and the gardens outside their doors. Landscapes now had a simplicity of line softened by the spilling greenery of shrubs and vines. Boulders and cobblestones were often used in walls, in steps and paths to link house and garden, and in vine-covered verandas created as cool, outdoor rooms. Although the gardens tended to include large front lawns, the guiding rule of landscape design was to work with the existing environment as much as possible, rather than impose an artificial order. In the bigger picture, the arts and crafts movement had an impact on the public realm as well, influencing people such as John Muir and other conservationists who played critical roles in the designation of Yosemite National Park.

At about the same time that Craftsman houses

THE LOVELACE GARDEN HAS THE SOFT LINES AND INFORMAL
STONEWORK THAT EXEMPLIFY THE NATURALISTIC STYLE.

were going up in view of Pasadena's Arroyo Seco, a growing interest in formal landscape design—especially in the traditional garden styles of Mediterranean countries—was taking hold in Santa Barbara and elsewhere around the state. Through the efforts of nurserymen and plant propagators, appropriate exotic and tropical plant material was already widely available; and after the 1913 opening of the Owens River Aqueduct eased the water shortage (at least in the Los Angeles basin; Santa Barbara and other areas continued to rely on local resources), an abundance of thirsty plants was made easier to maintain.

In the eyes of well-traveled and cultured new arrivals, California was the perfect place to replicate certain elements, or even overall designs, from great European gardens. These estate-builders wanted their landscapes to look mature immediately, perhaps as a way of lending their new lives an instant sense of history and permanence. Their aspirations created a demand for sophisticated designers who were well versed in classical tradition and could achieve the desired effects with plants appropriate to California.

Perhaps the best known of the early Mediterranean-style estates was El Fureidis. Inspired by a world tour undertaken by owner J. Waldron Gillespie and architect Bertram Goodhue, El Fureidis' construction was completed in 1906, and included a Roman villa surrounded by paths, walls, cypress *allées*, and reflecting pools characteristic of a Persian garden. In subsequent years, other equally grand and classically based estates were conceived by brilliant young landscape architects who successfully combined European training with local horticultural apprenticeships.

The most exciting period in California landscape history fell between World War I and the Great Depression. In 1916, San Francisco artist and designer Bruce Porter designed a sixteen-acre Italianate garden for Filoli, the Northern California estate of William Bourn II. Six years later, Anita Day Symmes Blake and her sister Mabel Symmes, a landscape architecture student at the University of California at Berkeley, created the Blake garden outside San Francisco.

In the Santa Barbara area, Lockwood de Forest designed equally dramatic landscapes combining classical influences with unexpected plant materials and a keen understanding for site. Ralph Stevens, son of nurseryman Kinton Stevens and de Forest's former employer, was another Santa Barbara master known for his enthusiasm for tropical plants and for creating the haunting world of Lotusland in Montecito. Dutchman Peter Riedel, at one time noted for his formal, Mediterranean-style landscapes, became an associate of Dr. Franceschi in the importation and cultivation of rare plants, and eventually ceased designing to become a respected horticultural consultant and teacher.

Other great designers of the time included Charles G. Adams, Wilber D. Cook, Jr., George D. Hall, Ralph Cornell, Katherine Bashford, Stephen Child, Lucile Council, A. E. Hanson, Edward Hunstman-Trout, Paul Thiene, Florence Yoch, and the Olmsteds of Boston. Along with Santa Barbara architects George Washington Smith and James Osborne Craig—who revived the Spanish Colonial style so appropriate to California—all created gardens that could be lived in, not simply enjoyed from

a distance. As with their Mediterranean models, these gardens contained the sights and sounds of water, shaded paths for wandering, and enclosed "rooms" for private retreat and contemplation.

While some estate construction continued into the 1930s and early 1940s, the Depression marked the end of most large-scale residential design. California's urban centers grew, but building lot sizes shrank and modest yet practical architectural styles such as Monterey Colonial became popular. An amalgam of adobe and redwood featuring arched, wraparound porches, the Monterey Colonial house usually had an East Coast–style landscape complete with roses, lawn, vines, and picket fence. Post-Depression years saw the rise of the small residential garden as a place for family gatherings, meals, sports, and children's play. As with residential styles of the time, garden design was streamlined by the influence of abstract art and the functional and modern movements in architecture.

During this period, the dominant figure on the landscape scene was Thomas Church of San Francisco. In 1955, he wrote *Gardens Are for People* to explain his concept of gardens appropriate to modern architecture. He popularized simple, flowing spaces that required minimal maintenance and catered to clients' needs rather than tradition. Church's designs emphasized functional considerations such as entertaining and lounging areas. He veered away from the naturalistic, seeing this style as inappropriate to small gardens that had to fulfill a variety of needs. In his view, a big lawn was a waste of usable space, but he also felt that formal, symmetrical design limited any of the aesthetic possibilities of a site.

While Church remained primarily a private gar-

THE OWNERS OF CASA DEL HERRERO TRAVELED TO SPAIN WITH ARCHITECT GEORGE WASHINGTON SMITH;
THERE, THE ALHAMBRA'S PEBBLEWORK INSPIRED THE INTRICATE PAVING DESIGNS OF THIS COURT.

den designer until he retired in 1977, a number of his notable colleagues in the field—Garrett Eckbo, Robert Royston, and Lawrence Halprin—branched out into planning public parks, plazas, universities, and commercial developments. Church and his peers had an enormous impact on modern garden design and helped make California a national center for landscape architecture.

In recent decades the rich and varied heritage of California garden design has been carried forward by new generations of landscape architects, designers, and horticulturalists. Combining a wide range of styles and experiences from the past with creative visions of the modern garden, contemporary designers aspire to a landscape practice aesthetically dynamic and responsive to the rapidly evolving context of California. These changing factors include population growth, resource scarcity, and the intricate ecological balance that governs not only our remaining "wild" areas, but also the shifting confluence of urban and wild that so characterizes California. As our awareness grows so too does our ability, as gardeners and as designers, to create gardens both rational and romantic, forward-looking and conscious of our historical inheritance, and ever closer to the Edenic dream that is the California garden.

OVERLEAF: THE VALENTINE GARDEN
IN THE SANTA YNEZ FOOTHILLS IS DESIGNED
FOR THE MODERN CALIFORNIA PRACTICE OF
YEAR-ROUND OUTDOOR LIVING.

the california garden

Spanish Beginnings
and Influence

CALIFORNIA GARDENS WERE born in the arcaded courtyards of the Spanish missions. Established in the eighteenth century by the Jesuit order as outposts of Spanish commerce, religion, and empire in the wild frontier lands of California, the missions were constructed in a series, each a day's march from the next, throughout the length of what the Spanish called Alta, or upper, California. Built with Native American labor under the supervision of the Jesuit padres, the missions were agriculturally self-sufficient communities that could accommodate, with a minimum of supply and interference from Spain, not only the billeting of soldiers and the dispatch of settlers, but the time-consuming primary task of the Jesuits: religious conversion of the native inhabitants. These isolated outposts were the only cultivated centers in a dry, harsh, and undeveloped land, offering travelers and settlers alike water, provisions, and protection from the sun. Inspired partly by the cloisters of Andalusia—a southern province in Spain whence came many of the early Spanish soldiers, priests, and administrators—and partly by the rugged Mexican farms they had passed through on their way north to California, the missions had thick, high walls to cast long shadows during the day's heat and colonnaded arcades to provide further protection from the elements. Yet while the basic forms were Hispanic, the mission structures and gardens were tailored to rugged pioneer conditions and were a far cry from their elaborate Spanish ancestors.

In Spain, both cultural preference and architectural practice had long favored the elaboration of interior private spaces over exterior public spaces. Residential architecture reserved adornment for private rather than public consumption: house facades were plain and white, with decoration reserved for interior space. Spanish gardens displayed a corresponding restraint. They reveled in greenery, accented not with bedded blooms but with *azulejos*—glazed, brightly colored tiles. Fragrance was valued more than floral color, although lavishly flowering vines and groups of blooming potted plants provided spots of living color amid the washes of green.

Spanish gardens were built as a series of patios divided by masonry walls, sometimes with windows to frame views. Patios were linked with straight, axial paths of glazed tiles, river rocks, or packed, colored earth. These paths often met in bubbling, trickling fountains that not only served domestic needs but also refreshed the spirit. Water was a precious commodity in Spain—particularly in the dry climate of Andalusia—and was symbolically celebrated in the garden. Artifice rather than nature thus ruled the Andalusian garden. The hand of the human creator was everywhere: in clipped box hedges and tiles, in walls, and in rills that guided, shaped, and cajoled nature into patterns pleasing to the eye.

Although mission buildings were inspired in part by these elegant Spanish forms, they also functioned as hastily erected frontier compounds organized for survival. Their courtyards may have suggested comfort and peace—particularly given the forbidding roughness of the local terrain—but they were utilitarian workplaces where bricks were made, hides tanned, equipment stored, livestock housed, and in some cases, residents slept.

Along with other mission structures, courtyards were built with scant resources and crude technology by padres, soldiers, and Native Americans equipped with more determination than know-how. Walls were constructed of baked mud bricks, thickly laid to support their own weight. Although roofs in some early missions were made of flammable thatched reeds, these were soon replaced by baked clay tiles of the type used in Spain. Ornamental Spanish details such as *azulejos* were unaffordable luxuries, but local artisans often painted accent lines and decorative motifs along the whitewashed walls and around the edges of fountains. Some missions also had carved wood benches and doors and occasionally, forged iron gates. A few had domes and simple bell towers, but for the most part the missions and their gardens were plain in the extreme.

One of the biggest distinctions between mission landscapes and

La Purísima's loggia provided shelter from the hot, dry summers and mild, rainy winters.

their Spanish precedents lay in the lack of any pleasure gardens within the California compounds. Despite primitive conditions, periodic droughts, floods, and earthquakes, residents raised food, tended livestock, and produced commercial commodities such as tallow, wine, and olive oil. Even in the best of times, water was a well-guarded resource to be saved for practical purposes.

As in the Spanish models, mission courtyards were structured around fountains or wells, but mission gardens were usually located at some distance from the courtyard. They were walled to keep out predators, and often vineyards, orchards, and vegetable gardens were cultivated separately. Some gardens had small areas for raising altar flowers, but it wasn't until after the Mexican government began its campaign to secularize church properties in 1830, crippling the missions by stripping away the vast agricultural landholdings which had sustained them over the centuries, that some of the remaining padres began planting their patios with edible and ornamental flora—perhaps for

solace as much as for actual sustenance.

After secularization destroyed the missions' capacity to sustain themselves, the mission system fell into decay and neglect. Yet even in their decline, the missions influenced the development of California's landscape. Throughout the nineteenth century these once-productive centers provided Mexican and American settlers with practical models for survival in its semi-arid conditions. Many of the simple early homesteads and larger, more elaborate ranchos were built in the plain, functional mission style, with home and farm structures arranged around a courtyard.

At the end of the century, just as unprecedented numbers of new immigrants were arriving from the East, bringing with them a taste for Victorian architecture and water-intensive gardens, a small group of Californians began to draw attention to the region's Spanish and Mexican heritage. Helen Hunt Jackson's romantic 1884 novel, *Ramona*, renewed interest in the old California idiom, as did newspaperman Charles Fletcher Lummis's magazine, *Land of Sunshine*. In 1888, Lummis's Landmarks Club began a campaign to save the decaying missions. Artists, too, "rediscovered" the missions in the early 1900s, and capturing them in colorful paintings, called further attention to their plight. Around the same time, San Diego architect Irving Gill, inspired by simple, bold mission forms, designed a series of austere and stunning residences, many of them built with drought-adapted gardens created by nurserywoman Kate Sessions.

In 1915, San Diego hosted the Panama-California Exposition, a promotional affair that became, under the architectural stewardship of Bertram Goodhue—a well-known California architect—a celebration of the Spanish Colonial Revival style. This gala event sparked a wave of all-out public enthusiasm and prompted designers and wealthy clients to travel to Spain for garden and architecture tours. Returning home, they created great Spanish-style estates, palatial homes set in elaborate gardens flavored by the Alcázar in Seville and the Gen-

eralife in Granada. Although they contained certain elements that were distinctly not Spanish, these estates, because of their scale and grandeur, had more of the opulent flavor of old Spain than did the missions.

With their plain, utilitarian style and economical forms and materials, the missions proposed garden living on a more modest scale. The impact of mission gardens on later generations of homeowners was based largely on seductive reconstructions that had little to do with the original landscapes. Creating lovely ornamental gardens with a mix of native plants and Mediterranean exotics, modern designers have added color and comfort to the austere framework of the original compounds, supporting a beloved myth about gracious, historic California. But while the restored mission compounds are sometimes more aesthetically pleasing than the grubby originals, they still recall California's early history, reminding us of the rich Hispanic heritage that provides us with some of the most appropriate models for western design.

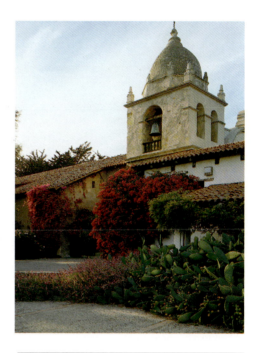

MISSION SAN CARLOS BORROMEO IS ONE OF THE FINEST SURVIVING EXAMPLES OF SPANISH COLONIAL DESIGN IN CALIFORNIA.

Mission La Purísima Concepción

Lompoc

BEYOND THE GRACEFUL colonnade at Mission La Purísima Concepción lies a large, open yard whose now-still fountain and rustling olive trees give little hint of this mission's eventful past. Dedicated in 1787, La Purísima, located four miles east of Lompoc, was quickly and crudely constructed and had to be rebuilt after its first few years of existence. Its second incarnation, of tile-roofed adobe, lasted a prosperous decade, during which the mission's population grew to more than 1,500 people and 20,000 livestock. After secularization had all but ruined the mission, it was sold in 1845 for $1,100 to one Don Juan Temple of Los Angeles. During the 1930s, the National Park Service spearheaded an effort to restore the mission, which eventually became the cornerstone of a 980-acre preserve that joined the State Park system in 1941.

Given the advanced state of La Purísima's decay, the National Park Service had to hire a specialized staff for extensive historical research. For the work of reconstruction, the Park Service engaged the aid of the Civilian Conservation Corps. When they began, very little remained of the mission complex beyond crumbling fragments of walls, the church floor, and parts of the water system. La Purísima had not been built on the typical courtyard plan, but as an open L, and by the thirties, whatever garden it might have once had was gone. Its scruffy grounds offered no means of determining what, if

THE PEACE NOW SURROUNDING THIS QUIET, OLIVE-SHADED FOUNTAIN IS FAR REMOVED FROM THE MISSION LA PURÍSIMA'S HARDSCRABBLE PAST.

A HEDGE OF PRICKLY PEAR CACTUS COMPLEMENTS THE AUSTERITY OF LA PURÍSIMA'S ARCHITECTURE.

anything, had ever grown in the five-acre area selected for landscaping, which centered around a vestigial fountain in front of the priests' residence.

To begin the process of creating an appropriate setting for the restored mission buildings, the National Park Service had a group of landscape architects—headed by Lewis Brandt of San Francisco—draw up a formal garden plan. An English horticulturist, Edwin D. Rowe, took charge of the planting, which, given the lack of reliable data, was to be visually pleasing rather than historically accurate.

Today, the grounds seem authentic. The features are spare, the planting quite simple. There is a quiet air of restraint about the place that goes well with the aura of a cloister. All that is missing—even from the plain, dirt yard that surrounds an igloo-shaped outdoor oven—is any hint of the desperate struggle to survive that was so much a part of California's mission life.

OPPOSITE, ABOVE: ONCE A BUSTLING MISSION, BETWEEN 1812 AND 1824 LA PURÍSIMA SUFFERED EARTHQUAKES, FLOODS, DROUGHTS, FIRES, AND REVOLTS THAT LEFT THE BUILDINGS DEVASTATED. OPPOSITE, BELOW: THE MISSION COURTYARDS WERE ORGANIZED FOR WORK RATHER THAN PLEASURE.

San Carlos Borromeo de Carmelo

Carmel

IN STRIKING CONTRAST TO the simplicity of La Purísima is the opulence of San Carlos Borromeo de Carmelo. Today, great masses of pink and blood-red bougainvillea climb its worn adobe walls, and Mexican bush sage (*Salvia leucantha*) runs in purple profusion. Mounds of prickly pear cactus (*Opuntia Ficus-indica*) and hydrangea, feathery olives, and a flaming field of montbretias proliferate where, in the mid-1800s, a scant twenty years after secularization, a ruined, almost roofless church stood alone on an empty plain. It was overrun with squirrels, cattle roamed through it, and the surrounding land right up to its walls had been sold for farming.

Founded in 1770 in Monterey by Father Junípero Serra, the Jesuit founder and administrator of the California missions, and relocated a year later to the nearby Carmel Valley, San Carlos was once a thriving, bustling place. The first seat of authority for the mission system, it was well located amid pine and cypress forests just five miles from the port of Monterey. At the peak of its influence in the early nineteenth century, San Carlos consisted of a large complex of buildings—church, living quarters, and workshops—around a spacious quadrangle. The church itself evolved from a log structure to the imposing stone edifice—complete with a Moorish-style bell tower—where Father Serra lies buried.

ONCE A RUINED HEAP BARELY STANDING IN THE MIDDLE OF FARM FIELDS, SAN CARLOS WAS RESTORED FIRST IN 1884, AND AGAIN BETWEEN 1931 AND 1939.

THANKS TO THE BLESSINGS OF CARMEL'S MILD COASTAL CLIMATE, THIRSTY IMPORTS
SUCH AS THIS HYDRANGEA THRIVE ALONGSIDE MORE DROUGHT-TOLERANT NATIVES.

First restored in 1884, in time for the centennial of Serra's death, the building had an inappropriately pitched, shingled roof for fifty years. The last effort at restoration, begun in 1931 by curator Harry Downie of the California State Park Service and lasting eight years, utilized archaeological and historical research to re-create as much as possible the mission in its heyday.

Downie worked on the gardens as well as the buildings over many years. Again, there were no records of the original gardens, if any existed, nor did Downie have any surviving trees or plants to work with. According to the mission's current curator, Richard Menn, Downie's garden "does not pretend to have an early California look, but was landscaped with beauty and color in mind."

The grounds blend California natives, Mexican imports, and sun-loving, drought-tolerant specimens from climates similar to Carmel's. The hardy mix goes well with red tiles and adobe, and suggests a certain life-affirming disarray. It seems just the kind of garden, in fact, that a cheerful, unworldly cleric might take it upon himself to plant.

OPPOSITE: THE GARDENS WERE RE-CREATED FOR
AESTHETICS RATHER THAN HISTORICAL ACCURACY.

Casa del Herrero

Montecito

IF THE MISSIONS EMBODIED a simple, functional version of Hispanic tradition, the 1920s-era estates of Santa Barbara and Montecito drew on more elaborate precedents for inspiration. Built after the Panama-California Exposition of 1915, Casa del Herrero in Montecito features elements from the Alcázar, the Alhambra, and the Generalife, and is thus supremely Spanish in feeling, while remaining true to the California landscape.

Even among other lavish Montecito estates, Casa del Herrero (which means "House of the Blacksmith") was notable for its attention to detail, and for the lengths to which its creators, George F. and Connie Howard Steedman, originally of St. Louis, went to design a world flavored by authentic Hispanic grandeur. At an early stage in the

design process, the Steedmans traveled to Spain with their architect, George Washington Smith, a proponent of Spanish Colonial Revival style, and with Mildred Stapley Byne and Arthur Byne, experts and writers on Spanish gardens.

Ralph Stevens, the son of prominent Montecito nurseryman Kinton Stevens, was the first landscape architect on the project, and his trademark preference for tropical plant material is especially evident. During the garden's twenty-year

ABOVE AND OPPOSITE: CASA DEL HERRERO, BUILT DURING THE HEYDAY OF ESTATE LANDSCAPE DESIGNING, RE-CREATES CALIFORNIA'S SPANISH HERITAGE ON A GRAND AND OPULENT SCALE.

ABOVE AND OPPOSITE: Colorful, finely detailed azulejos accent the prevailing green of the Steedman garden.

evolution, plantsman Peter Riedel offered his expertise as well. Landscape architects Lockwood de Forest and Francis Underhill—both noted more for their abstract, painterly compositions with plants than for any love of Spanish style—contributed further to the design.

Throughout the garden, classic Spanish tiles are used decoratively. Yet there is also, in the East Garden, a double mixed border of statice (*Limonium perezii*), agapanthus (*Agapanthus africanus*), calla lilies (*Zantedeschia aethiopica*), and Shasta daisies (*Chrysanthemum* x *superbum*) among other perennials and a generous sprinkling of annuals—a flowery feast that one wouldn't find in a Spanish landscape. Elsewhere, water bubbles and trickles in the dramatic, sparing Hispanic manner, drop by drop, into tiled pools. Appearing first in the octagonal foun-

tain of the motor court, the precious liquid seems to disappear beneath the house, only to reappear later in fountains, pools, and rills that shepherd it thriftily downhill to its final, shimmering performance amid cobalt-blue tiles. But along with the typical treatment of water, the garden also makes free-wheeling use of lawns, a thirsty element that would never have appeared in the landscapes of Granada or Seville. Neither would the otherworldly cactus garden, so suggestive of a western desert.

What the Spanish gardens would have shared with Casa del Herrero is the seductive progression from one intimate garden space to another: many of the home's interior rooms open onto enclosed patios which, in turn, lead outward, east and south, to other walled and hedged spaces. The sounds of water and the scents of flowers, as well as the entice-

ments of vistas glimpsed through gates or arches, encourage the wanderer to venture farther, through a carefully modulated yet magical world.

Like many others of their time and place, the St. Louis Steedmans gloried in what would grow in California: orange trees, bird-of-paradise (*Strelitzia reginae*), winter-blooming roses. Their garden reflects the dual nature of their setting—a coastal paradise on the edge of a desert. With the help of visionary designers who reveled in the shapes and textures of plants, they styled a uniquely California creation. It blends the traditions they brought along from their well-heeled midwestern past with the novelties of their adopted home. Casa del Herrero captures California's Hispanic heritage in a rich, romantic light, but it also reinvents history to its own opulent advantage.

OVERLEAF: WATER, BUBBLING FROM FOUNTAINS AND COURSING THROUGH TILED RILLS, IS A MOTIF THAT BINDS THE GARDEN SPACES OF CASA DEL HERRERO TOGETHER.

Cordell-Morton Garden

Marin County

BEFORE DESIGNING THIS Marin County house and garden, Tom Cordell and David Morton traveled up and down California, visiting missions and studying their practical functions. Other sources of courtyard-plan inspiration included the Cloisters Museum in New York, recreated in large part from medieval European monasteries, along with the gardens of Tuscan villas in Italy and General Vallejo's famous Petaluma, California, adobe. The result, built in 1989, is a 100-foot square courtyard garden linking two long, low corrugated metal buildings created for living and working. The elements of the courtyard are simple. At its heart is a raised reflecting pool constructed of the same cast concrete used in the narrow paths separating thirteen rectilinear planting beds. Like the mission fountains and cisterns, the pool surrounded by an arid margin of decomposed granite offers refreshment on hot, dry days. Its still waters also give back a view of the rugged, sloping hills that encircle the home with hulking majesty.

Six twenty-five-year-old transplanted olive trees accent the space at various points near the pool. A simple version of a mission-style arcade edges the entire courtyard, forming a sheltered walk in front of the two buildings and two more covered walks that connect them, thereby enclosing the space. Though walled on the exterior with the same

THE MISSION-INSPIRED CORDELL-MORTON HOUSE WAS DESIGNED AS A FUNCTIONAL COMPOUND MEANT TO BLEND IN WITH THE LOCAL CORRUGATED-METAL DAIRY BARNS. AT NIGHT, THE DOORS ARE SHUT TO PROTECT THE GARDEN WITHIN FROM FORAGING DEER.

industrial metal that covers the house, the two connecting links of the arcade feature sliding doors that open to views of rolling pastureland.

Cordell and Morton's combination of contemporary materials, warehouse-type architecture, and traditional California style offers privacy yet extends an openness to the outdoors—both cherished commodities of mission design.

CLOCKWISE THIS SPREAD: THE COMPOUND WHEN CLOSED SCARCELY HINTS AT THE HORTICULTURAL ARRAY WITHIN. IN ADDITION TO BLUEBERRIES, CURRANTS, GRAPES, PEACHES, AND NECTARINES, THE OWNERS GROW CACTI, SAGES, LAVENDERS, ROSEMARY, SANTOLINA, GERANIUMS, AND ROSES.

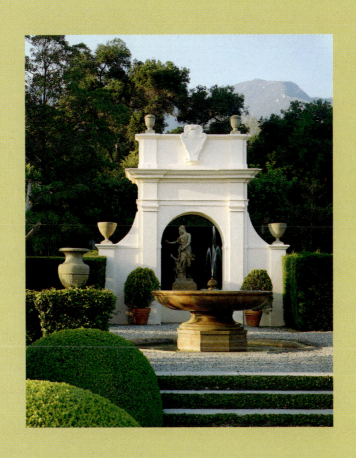

the classic garden

THE GOLDEN AGE
OF ESTATE GARDENS

The garden of Constantia in Montecito was designed for Arthur and Grace Meeker by Lockwood de Forest, who exploited the beauty of water to its fullest.

Originally a Montecito winter getaway, Val Verde and its gardens received a complete makeover by garden designer Lockwood de Forest.

aCROSS THE NATION, THE EARLY years of the twentieth century were a time of large-scale estate building: industrial magnates and those who had made fortunes in mining, banking, and transportation fled increasingly crowded, polluted cities for country life in such places as Long Island, Maine, and Newport, Rhode Island. Their new suburban manors and seasonal rural retreats eschewed the ornate, Victorian sensibilities of the late nineteenth century in favor of the classical aesthetic developed at the École des Beaux-Arts in Paris during the 1880s. Cultured and well traveled American estate-builders of this period understood and appreciated the Beaux Arts emphasis—so rooted in Greek and Roman ideals—regarding symmetry, harmony, and proportion.

By the dawn of the period known as the Golden Age of American Gardens—which ran from about 1900 to the early 1940s in California—designers and gardeners were also tiring of Victorian clutter and disorderly, naturalistic landscapes that bore no intimate connection to the houses they sur-

rounded. The excitement of plant collecting for its own sake was giving way to a desire to integrate specimen plants into more sophisticated, architecturally oriented designs.

California's estate-builders were eager to capture not just the actual form of the classical Mediterranean garden but its very soul, transported and enlarged. And so they grew both the familiar plants of the eastern American and European garden traditions and an array of extraordinary leafy wonders from around the globe. They designed sloping terraces, dramatic overlooks, and intimate seductions of water and fragrance that invited viewers to leave the house and take a leisurely stroll outside.

Yet of course, California was not Italy. It was the last of the American frontier, a young, dynamic society still in the process of creating itself. Thus, rather than simply duplicating what they had admired on their European tours, Californians embraced the uniqueness of their landscape.

While formal academic programs in garden design were almost nonexistent, early Cali-

New Yorker Lockwood de Forest's own garden in Santa Barbara combined classical lines with a subtly modulated play of space and color.

fornia garden designers were often as sophisticated as their clients. Francis Underhill, designer of such dramatic Santa Barbara–area estates as Arcady, was born into a well-to-do Long Island family and traveled widely in Europe with a cadre of tutors. Florence Yoch—known for her many Pasadena gardens as well as her work in the movie business (she designed sets for *Gone with the Wind*)—was the daughter of a wealthy Laguna Beach hotel owner. San Franciscan Bruce Porter, creator of Filoli's fanciful gardens in Woodside, was a painter, decorative artist, and one-time member of *Les Jeunes*, a circle of artists who sought to forge a style based on California's natural splendors and the aesthetic heritage of Europe. Lockwood de Forest, one of the most talented and visionary of the Golden Age designers, grew up in a cultivated New York family. He took landscape-design courses at Harvard and the University of California, had a brief apprenticeship with the landscape architect Ralph Stevens, and wandered through Italy and Spain studying gardens before opening his Santa Barbara practice in 1920.

These designers offered a broad, worldly perspective coupled with a sensitivity to California's unique conditions. In their hands, natural elements in the landscape found echoes in clipped hedges and expanses of glassy water; boundaries were rigidly set, then softened by spilling foliage; varied classical elements and allusions were everywhere, but expressed in exotic materials that made them unexpected and fresh.

Often featured on garden tours—which were attended by landscape lovers of humbler means as well as members of the local gentry—the estate gardens had an enormous impact on design layouts and plant choices of the day. The example set by the magnificent estates inspired the creation of many smaller Mediterranean gardens and laid the foundation for what has become an enduring and appropriate landscape style for the Golden State.

Florence Yoch designed Il Brolino in 1922, at the height of California's Golden Age of gardens.

Val Verde

Montecito

STANDING SENTRY ALONG the upper terrace at Val Verde is a line of matched columns whose capitals support nothing but sky. Tall, square, and more cleanly modern than the crusty, weatherworn house, they suggest something half finished, a polished ruin, a paradoxical mystery. Such arresting, unconventional detail is typical of the designs of Lockwood de Forest, who revamped the seventeen-acre Montecito enclave for his friend Wright Ludington.

Bertram Goodhue had designed Val Verde's rustic and rather plain Spanish-style house in 1915 for Henry Dater (cousin of New Yorker J. Waldron Gillespie, whose Santa Barbara house El Fureidis Goodhue had designed in 1901). In typical Beaux Arts fashion, Goodhue sited the house on a hill overlooking a stream and laid out garden terraces and a pool. Pasadena landscape architect Charles Gibbs Adams designed the original planting.

C. H. Ludington, Wright's father, a publishing executive from Philadelphia, bought the property from Dater in 1925. He hired de Forest to transform what had been a winter getaway into a year-round house, and to redesign the landscape so that it fit more smoothly into its setting. Over the next twenty years, working first for the elder Ludington and then with the active, involved Wright, de Forest dramatically altered the tone of Val Verde. He enlarged the house and built garages, replacing grassy terraces the Ludingtons considered dull with

LOCKWOOD DE FOREST, THE MOST TALENTED OF THE GOLDEN AGE DESIGNERS, COMBINED CLASSICAL ELEGANCE WITH A MODERN EDGE AT VAL VERDE.

The reflecting pool at Val Verde, with de Forest's marching columns visible beside the house.

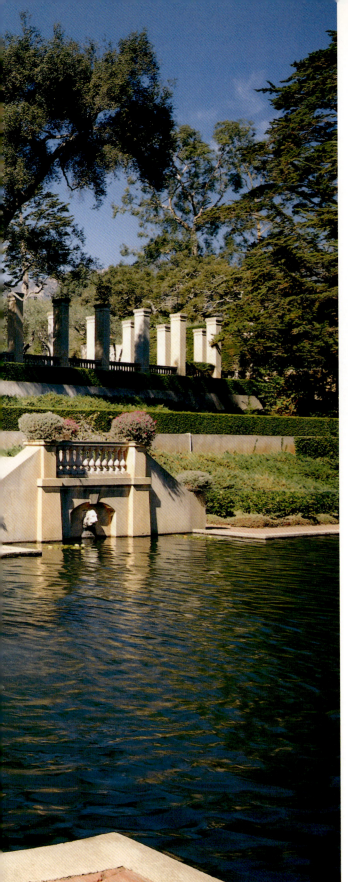

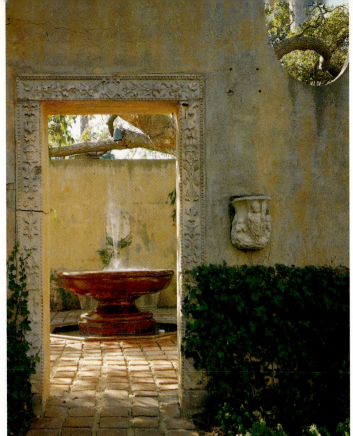

dramatic and more easily maintained reflecting pools. He converted a reservoir into a swimming pool, and added paths, fountains, walls, enclosed garden rooms, and a hilltop art gallery to house some of the Ludingtons' extensive collection of paintings and Greek and Roman statues.

In the process of remodeling, de Forest strengthened the axial quality of the landscape and opened the view to the ocean. He created a transitional space between the garden and its natural surroundings, and allowed the design—which was very formal close to the house—to become more relaxed as the paths wound down into a wooded area near the property line. He also borrowed from the wild landscape, integrating, for example, the towering presence of native evergreen coast live oaks (*Quercus agrifolia*) around the reflecting pools.

ABOVE: DE FOREST'S DESIGNS REVEAL THE PLEASURE HE TOOK IN WEAVING THE PRESENCE OF WATER INTO HIS GARDENS.

ABOVE: NATIVE OAKS CAST INTRICATE SHADOWS ON A SIDE COURT.

OPPOSITE: A FOUNTAIN NEARLY HIDDEN BY HEDGES TERMINATES A GARDEN PATH.

Throughout the garden, the gnarled meanderings of oak boughs are set off by more disciplined forms: squared-off box hedges, tall columns, Italian cypresses. On the east side of the house, clipped hedges and freestanding columns cast their elegant reflections into turquoise pools. Wide stone stairways adorned with potted succulents and rosemary lead downhill, away from the house, through several terraces marked by neat bright green Japanese box and rambling silver-green juniper.

De Forest capitalized on views and evoked particular moods in the garden to create special spaces for contemplation. Nor did he miss many opportunities to introduce the delightful music and mirroring qualities of water into his designs, whether by turning unused cisterns into yet more reflecting pools or by tucking an octagonal Spanish fountain into a bower of hedges overshadowed by palms.

In contrast to the lingering tendency toward overplanting that still characterized gardens of the twenties and thirties, de Forest's plant palette at Val Verde was simple. Instead of mixing a number of specimens in a single bed, he often used one plant in profusion, and relied on subtle foliage contrasts—scruffy silvers against sharp greens—for the power of his compositions.

REFLECTED IN AZURE POOLS, THE SENTINEL-LIKE COLUMNS AND FORMALLY CLIPPED HEDGES OF VAL VERDE
PLAY AGAINST THE LIVELY, GESTURAL FORMS OF MATURE OAKS.

Constantia
Montecito

SEVERAL YEARS INTO his work at Val Verde, Lockwood de Forest was handed another, very different sort of challenge. In 1930, Arthur and Grace Meeker of Chicago needed a landscape for the South African Dutch Colonial–style house that their son-in-law, Chicago architect Ambrose Cramer, was designing for them in Montecito. Relatively small by estate standards (3.2 acres), the Meeker property was well situated on a ridgetop and had both mountain and ocean views. But in the aftermath of the stock market crash of 1929, Meeker, who had both meat-packing and chemical businesses, experienced temporary financial worries that affected the plans for Constantia's garden.

It fell to de Forest to create a landscape worthy of a grand and, for Southern California, an unusually detailed house that recalled Cecil Rhodes's residence in Cape Town. The gardens needed to tie in with the architecture and appear larger than they actually were. Given the economic climate, they also had to be reasonably inexpensive to maintain.

In his customary style, de Forest focused on the splendor of the setting, calling attention to its stunning views and inviting them into his landscape. Again water was a favored tool, and he used it to magnificent effect, creating from a creekbed a single mirrorlike pool that captured mountains, trees, and sky. De Forest also recognized that in addition to its magical qualities, water required less effort to maintain than an equivalent expanse of lawn.

LOCKWOOD DE FOREST RELIED HEAVILY ON BLOOMING SOUTH AFRICAN PLANTS TO COMPLEMENT THE ARCHITECTURE OF CONSTANTIA.

Wherever he could, de Forest used plants native to South Africa—Cape pittosporum (*Pittosporum viridiflorum*), Cape honeysuckle (*Tecomaria capensis*), bird-of-paradise (*Strelitzia reginae*), lily-of-the-Nile (*Agapanthus africanus*), and sun-loving Transvaal daisies (*Gerbera jamesonii*). In other areas he compromised, using imported plants such as magnolia and jacaranda that happened to grow well in South Africa. And at the end of the pool nearest the house, he used a topiaried eugenia hedge to echo the building's Dutch Colonial–style roofline. At the pool's opposite end, the chunky forms of sheared black acacias (*A. melanoxylon*) appear to hover above the ground in a dotted line.

DE FOREST WAS EXCEPTIONALLY SKILLED AT MAXIMIZING THE QUALITIES OF A SITE, BY CREATING BOTH INTIMATE SPACES (ABOVE) AND EXPANSIVE VISTAS, BORROWING FROM DISTANT MOUNTAINS (LEFT).

De Forest Garden

Santa Barbara

LOCKWOOD DE FOREST was a master at shaping large-scale spaces, but he also created many gardens of more modest size. He favored simple yet unusual forms, played on the tension between wild and clipped foliage, and incorporated "borrowed" landscapes—such as the view of a distant mountain framed by trees—to make modest gardens seem larger. His own Santa Barbara garden—laid out between 1926 and 1927 around a small Romanesque villa he also designed—is a good example of de Forest's smaller gardens.

Initially, despite all his work for others, de Forest had a hard time settling on the right property for himself and his wife Elizabeth (who would later become a respected landscape architect in her own right). According to their son Kellam de Forest, his father's debate over where to live became a family legend: "He had his choice of a lot of properties," says the younger de Forest. "He looked at some in Hope Ranch, which he decided was too foggy. He rejected Montecito, maybe because it was too far out of town. He didn't want an ocean view—too distracting."

OPPOSITE: CLIPPED MYRTLE BALLS HELP DEFINE DE FOREST'S EXUBERANT PLANTINGS. ABOVE: ST. CATHERINE'S LACE BLOOMS IN THE COURTYARD.

GAZANIAS, IRIS, AND BABIANAS PEEK THROUGH ROUGH PAVING STONES
IN THE DE FOREST GARDEN.

Most important to de Forest were a view of the mountains and a mild climate, and he found the right combination at last in an area called Mission Canyon, near the Santa Barbara mission. Here he created a graceful compound focused on garden living. Every room of the house—now occupied by Kellam de Forest and his wife, Peggy—looks out on an intimate, secluded garden space. A central atrium accented by an almond tree and Persian tile work provides interior natural light. Outside, spilling plants smudge the lines of de Forest's clipped, formal garden structure, and tall trees frame a stunning view of Mission Ridge Peak.

Beginning with a property of about an acre, the de Forests increased the size of their garden in 1934, when they bought an adjacent lot to the east. Otherwise, says Kellam de Forest, the garden's structure has remained largely unchanged from its original design. What his parents experimented with over the years was the planting, playing with colors, shapes, and newly available materials. When his rose garden failed to thrive, for example, Lockwood de Forest moved the roses, replacing them with a solid field of lavender. While he was designing a Hope Ranch estate, he planted some of the same silver trees (*Leucodendron argenteum*) on his own property that he was installing there, to observe first-hand how they would grow. Similarly, he experimented with an exotic pink-blooming dombeya (*Dombeya* x *Cayeuxii*), training it to grow as a vine over the entrance of his house. And in a wild terrace above the house, he and Elizabeth tried many kinds of South African bulbs, including baboon flowers (*Babiana stricta*). Though at first these came up in a rainbow of colors, Elizabeth, through patient thinning, transformed them into a mass of periwinkle-blue.

In addition to being a learning lab, de Forest's landscape was also his demonstration garden for clients, a place to show off particular effects as well as plants that weren't readily available in nurseries. Kellam de Forest remembers his father leading such luminaries as Charles Laughton along the garden paths, pointing out certain features that might be appropriate in the landscapes he was designing for them.

OPPOSITE: A RARE SILVER TREE PRESIDES
IN THIS HERBACEOUS BED.

Il Brolino

Montecito

LIKE LOCKWOOD DE Forest, designer Florence Yoch paired formal elements with unbridled nature to interesting effect. She, too, had studied the great European gardens, and classical imagery appears often in her designs. An aged, established look appealed to her, and this was what she managed to create consistently for her clients in California.

Il Brolino, the seven-acre Montecito estate that Yoch designed for lumber heiress Mary Stewart in 1922, takes full advantage of both mountain and ocean vistas. Created to complement one of George Washington Smith's plain Italianate villas, the gardens range from an elaborate topiary parade ground—full of birds, swirls, egg baskets, and snow balls—to a circular terrace with benches and a craggy, off-center coast live oak (*Quercus agrifolia*).

The topiary wonderland, one of Yoch's best-known tableaux, reflects her characteristic perfectionism as well as the careful layering of forms in space that makes Il Brolino such a magical set piece. The tension between these clipped icons and the ragged magnificence of their surroundings sets the tone for the entire place.

In designing this garden, Yoch was faced with the dilemma of choosing forms that neither tried to compete with nor were totally dwarfed by the majesty of the setting. Living statuary proved an interesting choice. Its pairings of curved and straight lines evoke a sense of frozen movement while in the

FLORENCE YOCH WAS CELEBRATED FOR HER ABILITY TO ADAPT THE FORMAL EUROPEAN GARDEN IDIOM TO THE CALIFORNIA LANDSCAPE.

background, enormous, shaggy trees rustle and break up the light. Though topiary emphasizes the distinction between created and natural forms, it also connects them in a way a true sculpture garden couldn't.

Yoch designed Il Brolino during the early years of her career, at a time when the budgetary constraints of her clients often resulted in small-scale projects. While Mary Stewart and Il Brolino (which modestly, and rather ironically, means "The Little Garden") gave her a chance to spread her wings, she

adhered to the Mediterranean model and sculpted the space in discrete but connected rooms. Stealing some thunder from its monumental setting, the result is a landscape of many moods that delights in its parts and forms a satisfying whole.

OPPOSITE: YOCH BROUGHT HER EXPERIENCE IN DESIGNING EXTRAVAGANT MOVIE SETS TO HER GARDENS. ABOVE: WHIMSICAL TOPIARY SHAPES BALANCE THE CLASSICAL AUSTERITY OF AN ITALIAN CYPRESS.

Blake Garden

Kensington

WHILE LOCKWOOD DE FOREST and Florence Yoch were designing gardens around views of the Santa Ynez Mountains behind Santa Barbara, Anita Day Symmes Blake and her sister Mabel Symmes were busy in the hills above San Francisco Bay. There they created an epic Italianate landscape based on their shared obsession with exotic plants. Sprawling across eleven acres of a rugged, wind-blown slope, their garden captures an array of moods, from flowery expansiveness to somber formality to free-flowing naturalism. While it has been altered over the years—and renovated by the University of California at Berkeley's Department of Landscape Architecture, which now controls it—the property remains a striking example of its designers' unique vision.

Unlike other estate-builders farther south, the sisters were native Californians whose family had been located in the Bay Area for several decades. They also had strong ties with U.C. Berkeley, where Mabel Symmes was enrolled and studying landscape architecture while Anita Blake and her husband Anson were building their Mediterranean-style villa.

Designed in the early twenties by San Francisco architect Walker Bliss, the house (now the official

THE ELEVEN ACRES OF THE BLAKE GARDEN CONTAIN A RANGE OF MOODS: FROM THE SOMBER REFLECTING POOL (ABOVE), TO THE LIVING ABUNDANCE OF WILDFLOWERS BELOW ROCK OUTCROPPING (OPPOSITE).

residence of U.C. Berkeley's president) was positioned to command a sweeping bay view as well as to block the prevailing wind that rushes up the canyon from the water. Surrounded by tangled chaparral, the site has both wild and gentle areas, steep as well as rolling terrain, and features dramatic outcroppings of rock.

Symmes laid out the garden's architecture with an Italian-style water garden and reflecting pool, a vine-clad grotto, and a double curved staircase leading to a wild garden with a musical canopy of Eucalyptus. She also designed the walks, ponds, lawns, and innovative diamond-shaped beds that, when viewed from below, suggest waves of vegetation tumbling lazily downhill.

Anita Blake, much less interested in structure, worked on elaborate planting schemes. Though Symmes remained involved with the landscape long after she had finished her designs, it was Mrs. Blake

who worked in the garden almost every day for four decades. Contending with poor soil and destructive winds, she made her own compost and propagated seeds in a rundown glasshouse that once adjoined an old peacock run.

Interested in all manner of plants—especially those from other Mediterranean climates—she and her sister belonged to countless plant societies and exchanged seeds with other growers and plant collectors in the United States and abroad. As a result, the Blake garden gathered some 2,500 rare and unusual plants, and attracted considerable interest from nurserymen. Mrs. Blake would allow these professionals to visit the garden but refused to let them take any of her tempting specimens.

ABOVE AND OPPOSITE: A PROFUSION OF FOXGLOVES AND FORGET-ME-NOTS ENLIVENS THE FINELY SCALED SPACES OF THE BLAKE GARDEN.

"TIME BEGAN IN A GARDEN,"
reads the inscription on a sun-
dial in Filoli, located along
the San Francisco Peninsula
in Woodside and now open to
the public. There *is* something primeval about Filoli's
great monolithic yews, coast
live oaks (*Quercus agrifolia*), and the almost-cere-
monial seclusion of some of its garden rooms.

Filoli is based on a different aesthetic than many
of California's other large estates. Its original
owner, William Bourn II, was an ardent Anglo-
phile, and his forty-three-room brick house is in the
Georgian style, though borrowing details from other European traditions. The garden, with its spacious lawns, ordered flower beds, and walled rooms,
combines elements from nineteenth-century
England with those of the Italian renaissance.

Like the Blakes, Bourn was a native Californian
whose father had come to San Francisco from
Boston in the mid-1800s and made a Gold Rush
fortune. The Cambridge-educated Bourn took
over his father's gold mine and then had several
successes of his own. The name for his pastoral retreat was shorthand for his favorite heroic credo:
"FIght for a just cause, LOve your fellow man, LIve
a good life."

At the end of World War I, Bourn chose two
like-minded creative talents to help build Filoli.
Both architect Willis Polk and garden designer
Bruce Porter shared his fondness for the glories of

WILLIAM BOURN, THE ORIGINAL OWNER OF
FILOLI, WAS THE SON OF A GOLD RUSH
SPECULATOR. THIS GRAND SIXTEEN-ACRE GARDEN,
LOCATED ON THE SAN FRANCISCO PENINSULA,
IS NOW OPEN TO THE PUBLIC.

A robust climbing rose frames a doorway and softens Filoli's classic Georgian architecture.

A MAGNIFICENTLY ORCHESTRATED PROCESSION OF SHEARED FORMS MARCHES TOWARD THE DISTANCE.

California as filtered through the sophisticated prism of European tastes. Polk and Porter—former members of *Les Jeunes*—were friends of Bourn's, and Polk had already designed two other homes for him. An active, collaborative client, Bourn chose the lofty, oak-enclosed site for his home and determined that the natural hillside and lake vistas from his windows should dominate the garden views. In the Beaux Art manner, the house's major axis continues out into the garden, and there is an overall sense of unity between the building and its sixteen acres of formal landscape.

Porter's design was elaborate and architectural, relying on clipped trees and hedges, axial paths, and stone walls to shape the space. Among the most striking forms are the three hundred enormous Irish yews (*Taxus baccata*)—dark columns, rounded and flat-topped—that were raised from cuttings taken from an estate of Bourn's in Ireland. Never far from view at any point in the garden, they stand sentrylike at the entrance and form a moody *allée* along the southeast axis. While they are a brooding presence in the background of the sunken garden, the rose garden, and the knot garden (a later feature),

they have been invited into the walled garden, where they lurk like shy, oversized cousins among the delicate fruit trees and flowers.

Throughout the landscape, garden rooms are carefully composed and balanced, both within their own boundaries and in relation to the surrounding views. In the sunken garden, the boulderlike forms of silvery bush germander (*Teucrium fruticans*) anchor the corners of the reflecting pool and echo the silver of chunky olive trees, some inside the garden, some in the distance, beyond its hedged border.

The walled garden is a graceful, symmetrical assembly of austere and exuberant elements. Lawn terraces with low, curving walls descend beneath weeping trees to a round pool circled with potted petunias and a sea of lawn.

One of the most haunting of Filoli's garden rooms is the High Place, an elevated, semicircular space that terminates the axis of the yew *allée*. Enclosed by a tall, shadowy cypress hedge, the garden features a velvety lawn, benches, and wisteria-wrapped concrete columns that suggest a sacred ruin.

ABOVE: ELABORATELY COIFFED JUNIPERS ADD A TOUCH OF FORMALITY TO THE FILOLI ESTATE. OPPOSITE: POTS OVERFLOWING WITH PANSIES PROVIDE ACCENTS OF SUMMER COLOR.

ABOVE: WISTERIA FLOWERS ON CONCRETE COLUMNS.

OPPOSITE: A VIEW OF THE LAWN BETWEEN THE TWO BROODING ALLÉES OF IRISH YEWS.

the
wild
garden

NATURALISM IN DESIGN

GARDENERS HAVE ALWAYS debated whether to control nature or to let it run rampant; and thus, gardens range from landscapes that are as structured and contrived as architecture to untamed woods and flowery fields seemingly untouched by designing hands.

The looser, more organic approach to garden design has often emerged in reaction to a prevailing formal aesthetic. During the latter half of the nineteenth century in England—an era dominated by the artifice and opulence of the Victorian style and the gnashing machinery of the Industrial Revolution—horticulturist William Robinson spoke and wrote passionately about the glories of the English countryside. He proposed that English gardens eschew the tight formality and sheared topiary forms of the dominant French-influenced model then in vogue in favor of a looser, more bouyant style appropriated from nature. Celebrating native plants and naturalized ex-

otics, Robinson's wild garden was a free-flowing showcase for horticultural specimens then newly available in England.

Like its close cousin, the gentrified cottage garden, the Robinsonian landscape looked far more spontaneous than it actually was. A romantic, idealized wilderness, the wild garden was carefully planned and orchestrated—generally by sophisticated plantsmen—with an eye for well-integrated forms, textures, and colors.

In place of the straight lines of formal gardens, it featured paths and beds that followed the natural contours of the land, and luxuriant swaths of wildflowers that were allowed to seed freely and mingle in one another's territories. But the wild garden was lustier and flashier than anything found in nature. It blended plants that rarely, if ever, occurred together on their own; it was full of dramatic foliage contrasts, artificially created meadows, and forests strategically thinned to open up sunny glades for imported woodland flora.

In this country, and in California particularly, the wild gar-

WESTERN HILLS NURSERY
IN OCCIDENTAL BOASTS
A PROFUSION OF NATIVE AND
INTRODUCED PLANTS CAREFULLY
ARRANGED IN SMALL-SCALE
MICROCLIMATES.

den was taken up in a less elaborate form by members of the early twentieth-century arts and crafts movement. Sharing Robinson's reverence for nature, they constructed wooden Craftsman bungalows, with paths, wide porches, and stone walls. They also laid out flowery, overgrown gardens developed around existing trees and native plants. Though the Craftsman-style gardens did not often go so far as to relinquish the pleasure of a neatly mowed expanse of lawn, their *laissez-faire* use of large, ranging shrubs and dramatic jumbles of contrasting foilage and flowers pointed the direction for the wild gardens that would follow.

Like earlier proponents of Craftsman style, today's Californians are also seeking more appropriate garden models than those based on lawns and elaborate bedding schemes. In response to rampant development and an unstable water supply, there is a new interest in native plants and drought-tolerant exotics, and in creating informal, naturalistic gardens suitable for the climate and landscape.

Though partly a practical response to skyrocketing water bills, and partly an embrace of a more ecologically sound garden ethos, the use of native and drought-tolerant plants brings advantages from a design perspective as well. Being more closely adapted to the hot summers, wet winters, and long growing season of California, these plants require little seasonal cutting. Whether used to replace more thirsty species (for example, a low-maintenance Buffalo-grass lawn grown in place of traditional rye grass) or combined in massed plantings in an unirrigated "xeriscape" garden, the new plant palette lends itself to a looser, more fluid gardening style. The wild garden is a place for artfully letting things go, with less emphasis on structure and control, and with ample room for experimentation and unplanned change, as the plants themselves over time contribute their own suggestions to the evolution of the garden.

THE LOVELACE GARDEN, DESIGNED BY ISABELLE GREENE, ATTRACTS BUTTERFLIES THAT COMPLEMENT THE HOUSE'S BUTTERFLY MOTIFS DESIGNED IN 1923 BY ARCHITECT GEORGE WASHINGTON SMITH.

SIXTY MILES NORTHWEST of San Francisco, off a winding road heavily shaded by coastal redwoods, a wooden gate marks the entrance to Western Hills Nursery, the wonderful and eccentric business-*cum*-pleasure gardens of the late Marshall Olbrich and Lester Hawkins. During the early 1960s, when many city-dwelling Californians were threatening to move to the country and grow organic vegetables, Olbrich and Hawkins did just that. Leaving San Francisco, where they had lived for two decades—Olbrich as a philosophy professor and Hawkins as a teacher, musician, and taxi driver—the pair bought three hillside acres in Occidental, in an area surrounded by communes and back-to-the-land intellectuals.

To augment the existing coastal redwoods (*Sequoia sempervirens*) that framed their property, they first added European poplars (*Populus nigra* 'Italica') and other "romantic things," which, says California landscape designer Christine Rosmini, "they either cursed ever-afterward or took right out." Also on the list of the soon-replaced were rhododendrons, traditional woodland specimens that quickly lost their charm as the two explored more exotic possibilities.

OPPOSITE AND BELOW: IN THE SHADE OF TOWERING COASTAL REDWOODS, THE LANDSCAPE AT WESTERN HILLS SUPPORTS DIFFERENT KINDS OF VEGETATION IN EXOTIC, UNPREDICTABLE COMBINATIONS.

While both Olbrich and Hawkins had been interested in gardens before moving to Occidental, their new life revolved around studying and experimenting with plants. It was Olbrich's idea to set up a nursery to make their enterprise self-supporting. To learn the business, he worked at local nurseries, read extensively, and corresponded with horticulturists and designers. While taking on odd jobs and taxi driving for a living, Hawkins started laying out gardens on the hillside, an ongoing learning process that led to an eventual career as a landscape contractor and designer.

Throughout the nursery, which is still open to the public, are plants that Olbrich and Hawkins collected on their travels to Australia, Greece, the Balkans, and Morocco, among other far-flung places. Arranged in small-scale microclimates that support different kinds of vegetation, the landscape is bold and painterly in its colors, and sculptural in its contrasting textures. Yet everywhere, there is a careful balance between the overall visual effects of each area and the display of specimen plants, a design consideration Hawkins wrote about eloquently in his frequent articles for garden magazines.

ABOVE AND OPPOSITE: WANDERING PATHS CROSS AND RECROSS RIVULETS AND CHART A COURSE PAST A POND, MANZANITA GROVE, HERBACEOUS BORDER, GRAY GARDEN, SCREE GARDEN, AND A MEDITERRANEAN-STYLE SLOPE.

Rosmini Garden

Los Angeles

PARTS OF CHRISTINE ROSMINI'S Los Angeles landscape seem to have sprung full grown from a wild California hillside. In and around the spreading shade of old evergreens, exotic hellebores seem right at home beside native Douglas iris (*Iris Douglasiana*) selections, while extravagantly seeding euphorbias (*Euphorbia characias* 'wulfenii') have jumped paths and boldly infiltrated the territories of cardoon (*Cynara cardunculus*) and Jerusalem sage (*Phlomis fruticosa*). Turn a corner, however, and the world turns white. Iceberg roses (*Rosa* 'Iceberg'), nicotiana (*Nicotiana* hybrids), oak-leaf hydrangea (*Hydrangea quercifolia*), and *Geranium sanguineum* 'Album' gather in scrappy, snowy profusion around a pedestal bench and a broken concrete floor, creating a hushed formality that turns eerie in the moonlight.

Even the more orderly elements of her landscape are wild around the edges. A staircase Rosmini designed as an homage to the English garden at Tresco Abbey (on an island off the southwest coast of England) is a riot of crawling succulents and groundcovers that bubble up between the steps. And her trademark broken concrete walls suggest civilization shattered and overthrown by nature rather than the guiding hand of humans. What makes her garden world both soothing and coherent are the overarching evergreens; the curving, connecting paths; and the consistent threading of

EVEN THOUGH CHRISTINE ROSMINI'S GARDEN SEEMS HAPHAZARD, AREAS LIKE THIS WHITE GARDEN SHOW THE MASTERFUL HAND OF ITS CREATOR.

DECEPTIVELY RANDOM IN APPEARANCE, GARDENS SUCH AS THIS ONE ARE
COMPLEX, HIGH-MAINTENANCE AFFAIRS CARED FOR BY KNOWLEDGEABLE PLANTSPEOPLE.

silver-gray foliage among the spectrum of greens.

In general, Rosmini devotes a lot of attention to foliage color and shape. Like her mentors, Olbrich and Hawkins, she has a vast working knowledge of plants, and her enthusiasm has fueled the recent trend toward English perennial gardening in Southern California. The euphorbias that must have struck such an odd note when she first used them in her garden several years ago are not uncommon now in sophisticated landscapes, though some of her other choices still are.

The pink-blooming *Tabebuia avellanedae* tree that arches above the path to her front door, for example,

is rarely found in the suburban gardens of Los Angeles, nor is *Eupatorium sordidum*, the lavender shrub that grows along her dining terrace. Yet these and other exotica seem more than comfortable amid the Peruvian lilies (*Alstroemerias*), Santa Barbara daisies (*Erigeron karvinskianus*), and humble dusty-millers (*Centaurea cinerarias*) that also crowd into her teeming beds. Nature has the upper hand over artifice here, but nothing is truly running wild.

OPPOSITE: THE LAVENDER AND YELLOW
TRUMPET FLOWERS OF TABEBUIA AVELLANEDAE
BLOOM ABOVE PHLOMIS AND EUPHORBIAS.

Lovelace Garden

Montecito

ON THE PRIVATE ESTATE of Jon and Lillian Lovelace in Montecito, four rolling acres of oak woodland surround an English-style house designed in 1923 by architect George Washington Smith. Garden areas, though rather shaggy and informal, are clearly man-made. Not so clear are the origins of the mounded purple-blooming periwinkle (*Vinca major*), wild *Senecio mandraliscae*, honeysuckle (*Lonicera japonica*), or the swirling nasturtiums (*Tropaeolum majus*) catching at the trunks of California live oaks.

The rustic pool was designed by Santa Barbara landscape architect Isabelle Greene, but the nearby drifts of flowers have simply seeded themselves—and continue to do so in even greater profusion at the wilder reaches of the property. As the land slopes downhill, away from the house and toward a dense enclosure of trees, the vegetation begins encroaching on paths carpeted with fallen leaves. Wildflowers, native oaks, and huge local sandstone boulders are the unifying themes of this wandering landscape, which, though far from domesticated, seems gently disposed toward humans.

ABOVE: ISABELLE GREENE'S ROMANTIC PLANTINGS FOR JON AND LILLIAN LOVELACE EMBRACE THEIR ENGLISH-STYLE COTTAGE DESIGNED IN 1923. OPPOSITE: PATHS CONNECT A CANOPY OF OAKS AND TREE STUMPS ENGULFED IN NASTURTIUMS.

GREENE DESIGNED THE SHAPE
OF THIS RUSTIC POOL BY
FOLLOWING THE DRIP LINES
OF SURROUNDING TREES.
PLANTINGS AGAIN RUN WILD A
SHORT DISTANCE FROM THE
POOL'S OUTLINING BOULDERS.

Slater
Garden

Santa Barbara

THE MEANDERING COBBLE-
stone walk that leads to Bill
Slater's Santa Barbara house
suggests, perhaps, a road to
heaven. Its allure combines
the immediate visual impact
of lavish, mosaic plantings—lavender, iris, statice,
and silver groundcovers beneath an olive tree—with
the sense of mysteries behind a walled court.

The garden was created by landscape designer
Dennis Shaw and unfolds in a series of discrete outdoor rooms, each with a distinctive flavor but linked
to the others through shared colors, forms, and
planting themes. There is a courtyard off the living
room, an entry terrace with a raised reflecting pool,
a fern court, and a dining terrace behind the house.
At the property's wilder reaches, an orchard grows
beside a picturesque dry
creekbed, and a rugged
slope displays a bristling,
rambling tapestry of dry,
flowering plants. To con-
nect all of the varied spaces,
Shaw used a mix of drought-tolerant evergreen
shrubs that bloom in a palette of blue, pink, violet,
yellow, and white. Rosemary and lavender appear
repeatedly with a shifting array of partners, the
thirstier selections installed close to the house, the
dryland plants elsewhere.

On the slope that leads down to the entry court,
for example, the dark green of rosemary blends first
into the lighter green of Jerusalem sage (*Phlomis
fruticosa*) and then with the silver grays of artemisia
and lavender. Yellow-blooming Jerusalem sage,

OPPOSITE: DENNIS SHAW CREATED THIS FLOWER-LINED PATH AS A SEDUCTIVE ENTRANCE TO BILL
SLATER'S SANTA BARBARA HOME. BELOW: THE ENTRY COURT IS ONE OF SEVERAL GARDEN ROOMS.

California poppies (*Eschscholzia californica*), and kangaroo-paws (*Anigoz anthos flavidos*) splash the landscape with color. On the back terrace lavenders and rosemaries are paired with roses ('Iceberg,' 'The Fairy,' and *Rosa banksiae* 'Lutea') and small trees create a fragrant, private enclosure.

But for all the dramatic effusiveness of the courts and terraces near the house, the hillside below is where the garden breaks free and its themes run rampant. Here, such things as *Artemisia* 'Powis Castle', a plump native sage (*Salvia clevelandii* 'Alan Chickering'), and blue hibiscus (*Alyogyne Huegelii*) scramble and billow hugely among the familiar lavenders, which, themselves unrestrained, grow exuberantly to boulder size.

This contrived, colorful wilderness implies a spatial continuum that includes home, gardens, and surrounding territories. It delights in abstract volumes of plants and the sensation they make when layered, painted, and daubed on in naturalistic profusion. This slice of nature dressed up by art goes one step further in catering to current environmental considerations: in the Slater garden, hardy plants subsist on rain alone.

ABOVE: PLANTS THAT REQUIRE WATERING, LIKE THESE ROSES, ARE PLANTED CLOSE TO THE HOUSE.
OPPOSITE: THE HILLSIDE BELOW THE HOUSE FEATURES PLANTS THAT REQUIRE LITTLE MAINTENANCE AND NO EXTRA WATERING.

the cottage garden

VARIATIONS ON A
TIMELESS THEME

An iris-lined rill in Nancy Power's garden.

A Reed bench occupies a shady spot beneath a crabapple tree in Richard and Doreen Hamilton's garden.

a T THE END OF THE NINETEENTH century, newly arrived Californians taunted their East Coast friends with photos of spilling roses and ripe oranges growing in their sunny winter gardens. Such a mix of the ornamental and the edible—with an emphasis on flowery profusion—is the essence of the cottage garden, a style most often associated with England but one that is probably as old as gardening itself. The Roman historian Pliny the Elder refers to gardens in Pompeii, describing courtyards in which pomegranates and figs grew side by side with oleanders, carnations, roses, and lilies.

Throughout history and across cultures, wherever people have had a bit of ground to call their own, cottage gardens have sprung up as a simple means of supplementing meager diets and beautifying surroundings. Early efforts were practical rather than ornamental—back-door kitchen plots where herbs, vegetables, and a fruit tree or two were crammed together with little thought for design.

Edgings, paths, and walls were simple, made of local stone or brick, and flowers crept in slowly, at first only in the useful form of blooming herbs.

Native plants were another part of the tradition since the gardens of poor cottagers depended upon what plants they could collect in the wild or beg from monasteries or manor gardens. The first true English cottage gardens began around the fourteenth century, and were modest plots containing old-fashioned plants no longer wanted by trend-conscious gentlefolk. Indeed, as more and more nurserymen began to grow and sell hybridized plants during the seventeenth century, cottagers unintentionally became the preservationists of old varieties that would otherwise have been lost. A century later, it was their very quaintness that led to cottage gardens' being idealized and emulated by more comfortable, middle-class garden builders.

Ultimately, the lack of style evident in cottage gardens became a style in itself. As with the mission gardens, later re-creations and revisions of the form have had more impact than the plain, utilitarian originals. A version of the cottage garden aesthetic began to turn up in great estates of the early 1900s (such as Hidcote in England), while, conversely, certain features from large-scale formal landscapes—rock gardens and herbaceous borders—appeared in cottage plots.

In marked contrast to the orderly hedges and color fields of more formal gardens, cottage landscapes have a characteristic informality, a "one of this, one of that" quality that expresses the particular tastes (and sometimes eccentricities) of their owners. In fact, this very personal aspect is what makes them so charming. With great intimacy, they reflect the loving hands that tend them. In recent years, as more people have taken up gardening, the cottage aesthetic has grown in popularity. It is often the style of choice for avid gardeners, who relish its heavy maintenance needs and enjoy experimenting with plants for their own pleasure rather than for the sake of trends.

California's cottage gardens are as eclectic and variable as its architecture, which, of course, features few true cottages. Ideally suited to the small lots that abound where real estate is quite costly, the packed beds and colorful jumble of the style surround Spanish Colonial homes, beach bungalows, and ranch houses. In the West, where traditions are freely mixed and appropriated, cottage gardens may feature Mediterranean courtyards, fountains, tropical plants, and California natives in English-style perennial beds. The region's Mediterranean flavor, its rich, exotic plant palette, and its almost year-round blooming season give its cottage landscape the distinctive charm that has appealed to garden lovers ever since the Victorian days of roses and citrus.

Today, the cottage aesthetic is being embraced as an inviting way to turn underused spaces—such as water-intensive front lawns—into intimate and colorful garden rooms.

THE SHEER EXUBERANCE OF THE COTTAGE GARDEN IS CLEARLY EVIDENT IN THE TREFETHENS' ST. HELENA GARDEN.

THE INFORMAL PROFUSION OF FLOWERS THAT CHARACTERIZES THE COTTAGE STYLE OF THE BANNING GARDEN IS WELL SUITED TO THOSE WHO LOVE PLANTS AND ENJOY TAKING CARE OF THEM.

Hamilton Garden

Pasadena

LANDSCAPE ARCHITECT Florence Yoch and her partner Lucile Council may not have been known for English cottage gardens, but their 1937 landscape for Sherman Asche's home in Pasadena included a charming, cascading flower show full of roses, Carolina jasmine (*Gelsemium sempervirens*), and other cottage favorites. Perennials overflowed the mortared flagstone walls of Italianate terraces, and Yoch's design also featured a citrus orchard with a backdrop of Canary Island pines (*Pinus canariensis*).

If anything, the garden is even lusher now than in Yoch's day. In 1989 and 1990, owner Richard Hamilton hired landscape architect Robert Fletcher to refurbish some of the herbaceous beds. Even the stairs rising from terrace to terrace are crowded with blooms from pots of daffodils, pansies, and primroses.

The borders themselves feature more daffodils,

LEFT AND BELOW: THE GENIUS OF THE HAMILTON GARDEN, WITH ITS HARMONIOUS BLEND OF STYLES, LIES IN ITS COTTAGE-STYLE MULTITUDE OF PLANTS.

rustling delphiniums, ranks of columbine, ranunculus, and Iceland poppies, all interspersed among torrents of roses. Rising in the background, a miniature grove of limes, lemons, and oranges adds its leafy abundance and fragrance. It also places the splashy cottage elements in a familiar California light: here are the very roses and citrus trees that so moved the state's earlier settlers.

As for the terracing, it is a time-honored way of squeezing more gardening or farming space out of a hillside, but in Yoch's hands it adds elegance and order to a characteristically disordered garden style. The straight walls and paths—not to mention the geometric volumes of lawn and brick patio below— make the verdant overgrowth easier to read. And the ascending steps and layered flower banks lead the eye up to the magnificence of shaggy pines against the sky.

RIGHT AND BELOW: A TUMULT OF COLOR FILLS THE HERBACEOUS BEDS BELOW AN ORCHARD OF FRAGRANT MIXED CITRUS TREES.

Power Garden

Santa Monica

MY OWN GARDEN IN Santa Monica is an example of a cottage-style garden freely interpreted. With its clipped hedges, stucco walls, tiled courtyard, and room-oriented layout, it might at first glance bear more resemblance to an enclosed Mediterranean garden. The original English cottagers never gardened in rooms, nor did they have any use for pergolas, reflecting pools, or *claire-voie* windows, all of which are present in this design.

I designed my garden over a period of ten years, beginning with the entrance and courtyard: these are now the primary areas for my outdoor entertaining. The courtyard's Mediterranean feel was dictated both by the Spanish style of the house and the appropriateness of the aesthetic to California's climate and year-round, indoor-outdoor way of life. Complete with olive tree, high retaining walls, and drifts of bougainvillea and juniper, the space has a raised pool filled with brightly colored koi fish and a large fireplace that provides heat for nighttime parties. There are chairs and tables for lounging and eating, and a number of potted, blooming plants grouped together, in the Spanish manner, on the tiled ground near the pond. The enclosure of the front gardens was based on more than a simple urge for privacy; it made sense

NANCY POWER TURNED A CONVENTIONAL, UNUSED FRONT LAWN INTO A SECLUDED SUNKEN GARDEN FILLED WITH TRADITIONAL COTTAGE GARDEN PLANTS.

for the full utilization of every inch of a small and narrow (50 × 160 foot) lot.

To link the front gardens to a studio, terrace, and garden behind the house, I replaced an existing driveway with a path of river rock and concrete aggregate hedged with rosemary and agapanthus. The back garden—which is also conveniently close to the kitchen door—is pervaded by the spirit of the age-old cottage landscape. In it, an upright rosemary goes cheek-by-jowl with unruly tomato plants, and spiky artichokes share space with Spanish lavender (*Lavandula Stoechas*). Beneath a spreading fig tree and billowy Bonica roses, the silver-leafed *Artemisia* 'Powis Castle' (a medicinal herb) mingles with the rich green of look-alike *Geranium incanum*. Here, too, is the delicate rue (*Ruta graveolens*), another medicinal herb from medieval times, alongside a robust family of hen and chicks (*Echeveria* x *imbricata*). Nearby, under a very large New Zealand flax (*Phormium tenax*) and the weeping, multihued foliage of a young Kashmir cypress (*Cupressus cashmeriana*), more herbs—sage, arugula, tarragon, and chives—grow tall for the picking.

Extending outward from the master bedroom is a small, sunny sitting terrace, also made of brown river rocks that are set in patterns into concrete. In the back, I had modeled a simple fountain after one seen in Pompeii, and edged a rill with *Senecio mandraliscae* mixed with purple irises plucked from an old California estate garden. The Mediterranean flavor of this feature is one of the many details that helps to give my cottage garden a distinctly California cast.

THE BRICK ENTRY PATH IS SOFTENED BY COLORFUL AND FRAGRANT MOUNDS OF LAVENDER, ROSEMARY, AND HELICHRYSUM.

ON THIS PAGE: VIEWS FROM THE STUDIO
INCLUDE THE WINDOW INTO THE SECRET GARDEN
(TOP); THE WILD HERB GARDEN (RIGHT); AND
SUCCULENT BORDERS (BELOW). OPPOSITE:
THE CENTER OF THE HOUSE AND GARDEN IS THE
COURTYARD.

Trefethen Garden

St. Helena

THE LUSH GARDEN OF JOHN and Janet Trefethen in St. Helena offers an alternative form of the classic cottage style in its flower-edged, Mediterranean-flavored front garden. The Trefethens are owners of a winery and live in the midst of sprawling family vineyards, although their property slopes up into the hills of the Mayacamas range. From the front of their ranch-style house, they look out on gentle mountains covered with native oaks (*Quercus lobata*), as well as acres of grapes, while the back of the house commands a sweeping valley view.

In 1983 the Trefethens began working with St. Helena–based garden designer Roger Warner to develop the entry courtyard into a secluded yet welcoming place of arrival, separate from the vineyard, but very much related in tone. Silver-gray olive trees planted along the garden's perimeter provide a fine feathery enclosure and also look stunning against the darker, denser oaks. The combination of the two, together with the green hills that turn so rapidly to gold in the summer, makes for an archetypal California view, colorfully augmented by the purples, blues, pinks, and whites of a spirited mixed flower border. Mounds of enchanting pink Felicia roses tumble on to the path toward sprigs of catmint (*Nepeta* x *Faassenii*), while *Ajuga reptans*, a hearty, dark green groundcover, seeps out of its bed, only to disappear before irre-

PINK FELICIA ROSES AND FOXGLOVES OVERFLOW STRAIGHT WALKS OF CRUSHED SHALE IN THE TREFETHENS' GARDEN.

pressibly popping up once again across the way.

Hellebores, foxgloves, veronicas, and phlox appear in great profusion in the landscape, and their lively color shows are supplemented by the annual planting of pansies, snapdragons, Iceland poppies, and primroses. There is also a generous sprinkling of exotics, such as various meadow rues native to the Himalayas. Herbs such as basil, oregano, burnet, parsley, marjoram, and lavender—many of which flower in summer and seed themselves throughout the garden—thrive among other drought-tolerant blooming plants such as penstemon, rosemary (*Rosmarinus officinalis*), and loosestrife (*Lysimachia punctata*). Just beyond the garden's edges are sloping banks of manzanita, ceanothus, and madrone (*Arbutus Menziesii*)—hearty natives that create a pleasing transition from the naturalistic formal landscape to the oak-clad mountains that so dominate the spirit of the place.

LEFT AND ABOVE: WITH ITS FRAMEWORK OF OLIVE TREES AND FLOWERING SHRUBS, THE TREFETHEN GARDEN SUGGESTS A MEDITERRANEAN RATHER THAN AN ENGLISH AESTHETIC, A CHARACTERISTIC OF THE CALIFORNIA COTTAGE GARDEN.

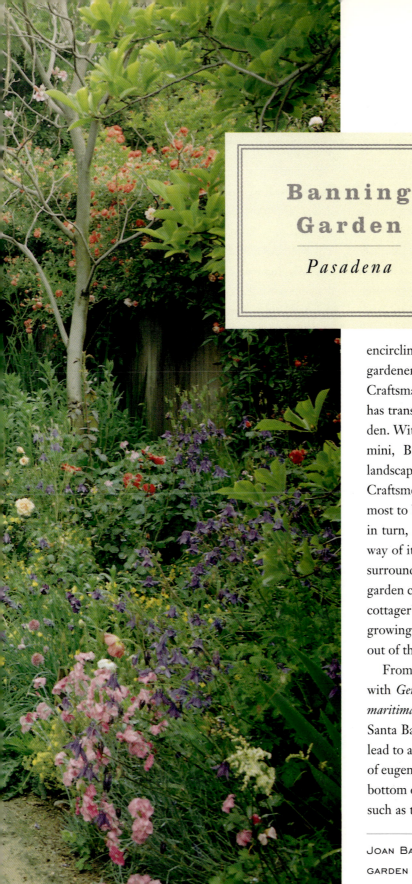

Banning Garden

Pasadena

PASADENA, JUST LIKE SANTA Barbara, has a particularly rich landscape tradition, and it has long been recognized for the beauty of both its historic estate gardens and the charming, flower-filled yards encircling its smaller homes. Joan Banning, an avid gardener and longtime resident of Pasadena, has a Craftsman house on a modest suburban lot that she has transformed into a stunning cottage-style garden. With the guidance of designer Christine Rosmini, Banning has created a lush, naturalistic landscape like those favored by early California Craftsmen. The vine-covered house appears almost to be growing out of the front garden which, in turn, seems to be spilling up into the house by way of its generous covered porches. A raised bed surrounds part of the structure, again bringing the garden closer to the indoors and also reflecting the cottager's goal of using every inch of available growing ground, even if that means conjuring it up out of thin air.

From the house, stairs of broken concrete burst with *Geranium incanum*, sweet alyssum (*Lobularia maritima*), common thrift (*Armeria maritima*), and Santa Barbara daisies (*Erigeron karvinskianus*), and lead to a swath of lawn. Potted topiary birds, made of eugenia, stand like whimsical, leafy guards at the bottom of the main garden steps. (Simple topiaries such as these often showed up in the seventeenth-

JOAN BANNING'S PASADENA COTTAGE GARDEN UTILIZES EVERY INCH OF GROWING SPACE AROUND HER CRAFTSMAN-STYLE HOUSE.

century cottage gardens of England, probably via the head gardeners of country estates who passed the skill on to cottager friends.)

Elsewhere in Banning's landscape, a long path of decomposed granite provides a foil for the every-which-way floral spray of an explosive double border. Repeating plant material holds the extravagant show together: the purple-blue columbine so popular in Pasadena gardens; pink dianthus with its silvery foliage; the pale green Pride of Madeira (*Echium fastuosum*) omnipresent in English perennial borders; and a white form of that old cottage favorite, Maltese-cross (*Lychnis chalcedonica*). All of this is banked by a spill of roses—yellow, red, and pink—and the path that runs through it terminates in a single, stately white column, another point of

order in a wild world. In the cottage tradition, the front garden is visible from the street yet has a comfortable feeling of enclosure provided by a low hedge, climbing roses, and cascading vines.

Banning's landscape is formed by her knowledge as a plantswoman and by the boldness and idiosyncrasies of her taste. A gardener since 1955, Banning develops and changes her garden over time. Once she had ponds, but when raccoons repeatedly ate the fish, she had the ponds filled in. Now she simply has plants—colorful torrents of them—and plants, after all, are what she loves.

CHARMING DETAILS ABOUND IN THE GARDEN, SUCH AS TOPIARY BIRDS (BELOW), AND A WELSH CORN-CRIB SURROUNDED BY FLOWERS (OPPOSITE).

Chandler Garden

Santa Monica

MASTER LANDSCAPE DESIGNER Philip Chandler has carved an irresistible doll's garden from the scrap of ground that surrounds his Santa Monica apartment building. In lieu of the palms and multicolored impatiens packed around the apartments of his neighbors, his plein-air retreat is guarded by a stately gum tree (*Eucalyptus gunnii*) and features swirling bronze, silver, and blue-green foliage, a moodful complement to the frequent local fog.

Chandler, a preeminent Los Angeles horticulturalist, designer, and teacher, has inspired several generations of students and professionals with his impassioned views on California gardens. Yellow-green plants, he believes, have no place in a state whose natural hues are dusky olives, grays, and ochers. Plants that need too much water must be shunned. Lawns belong in a moist climate like England's, not in dry California.

Although his courtyard is only thirty-five feet square, Chandler has fit into it all the elements of a great garden: strong geometry, a vista, a water feature, and the comforts of seclusion. A mixed-shrub hedge shields it from the street; gravel and cement paths define its framework; a stone water trough reflects the sky; and there is a small, compelling view of the outside world through its low, iron gate.

But inside, against the backdrop of a tapestry hedge—*Pittosporum crassifolium*, purple hop bush (*Dodonaea viscosa* 'Purpurea'), silverberry (*Elaeagnus*

WITH A TRUE PLANTSMAN'S EYE, PHILIP CHANDLER TRANSFORMED THE COURTYARD OF HIS SANTA MONICA APARTMENT INTO A TAPESTRY OF GRAY, GREEN, AND BRONZE.

A BENCH NESTLES IN A POTTED SYMPHONY OF STRAP-LEAVED SUCCULENTS AND NEW ZEALAND FLAX.

CHANDLER'S GENIUS LIES IN COMBINING COMMON PLANTS
WITH THE RARE TO CREATE SUBLIME CONTRASTS OF COLOR AND FOLIAGE.

pungens 'Fruitlandii'), and pineapple guava (*Feijoa sellowiana*)—the real drama unfolds, in broad sweeps and tiny vignettes. Here, the plants provide the architecture: the walls and washes, the mounds and spikes that build on each other to create a dense and captivating visual field. Shaggy, midsize shrubs such as *Leptospermum laevigatum* 'Reevesii' and *Westringia rosmariniformis* contrast pleasingly with the bronze swords of New Zealand flax (*Phormium tenax* 'atropurpureum'), while periwinkle-blue baboon flowers (*Babiana stricta*)—a gift to Chandler from Elizabeth de Forest—spread their shadowy carpet below. Sea lavender (*Limonium perezii*) sprays purple above wandering streams of sharp blue-green *Senecio mandraliscae*, which are punctuated by the rounded black forms of *Aeonium arboreum* 'Zwartkop' and cabbagelike echeverias.

More pots in and around the garden hold overflow plants, which Chandler has no other space for. Two of his favorite trees—*Magnolia grandiflora* 'Little Gem' and *Podocarpus gracilior*—normally too large for a garden this size, are contained in this way, as are some oddly shaped succulents and bronze grasses (*Pennisetum setaceum* 'Rubrum'), which add more texture and form to the mix.

Chandler's own garden reflects his tireless enthusiasm and his appetite for experiments. Now in his eighties, he works outdoors almost daily, fiddling, changing plants around, moving in a flashy can-canning chorus of pink lisianthus (*Eustoma grandiflorum*) when things threaten to get dull. Alive with the potent visions of a horticultural artist, Chandler's tiny Eden is proof that you don't need an estate to garden like a king.

Tisch Garden

Los Angeles

THE STRAIGHT, CLEAN lines of a Craftsman house present an inviting framework for an uninhibited garden, as the members of the California arts and crafts movement well knew. Their vine-swathed homes seemed to grow out of the wild landscape, which generally they tried to leave as natural as possible. In contrast, my own version of a spirited Craftsman garden was based not on any natural model but on the architecture of plants carefully chosen and placed for impressionistic effect.

The location was a secluded spot in Rustic Canyon; the house was a small, early Craftsman bungalow whose owner, Patsy Tisch, had planned to enlarge but ended up redoing altogether with Los Angeles designer Don Umemoto. In addition to creating a new home in the style and vocabulary of the old, Umemoto, with the client, chose the color for the buildings and designed many of the elements of the property. My task was to make a garden that did the house justice, showing a corresponding attention to detail while also seeking new ground.

Patty Tisch is horticulturally knowledgeable and has an interest in uncommon plants. She encouraged me to pull out all the stops and come up with unexpected colors and patterns. I did: the garden is awash in surprising shades of aubergine and antique yellow foliage, brown and green flowers, and such favorites of mine as helichrysum limelight under-

A STYLIZED DESCENDANT OF THE CRAFTSMAN TRA-DITION, THE TISCH GARDEN IS AN IMPRESSIONISTIC MIX OF PATTERNS, COLORS, AND TEXTURES.

THE BOLD PATTERNS OF THE ENTRY COURT ARE MATCHED
BY THE STRIKING FOLIAGE OF NEW ZEALAND FLAX AND MAHONIA LOMARIIFOLIA

planted with black pansies. I've used some wonderful old California materials: cup-of-gold vine (*Solandra maxima*) and bronze cordyline (*C. australis* 'atropurpurea') are combined with drought-tolerant exotics like Pride of Madeira (*Echium fastuosum*) and *Mahonia lomariifolia*.

In assembling my plant collage, I did something I rarely do: I worked without a plan, making trips to the site with two or three plants to try them out together in a particular spot. It was very much a layering and editing process, undertaken against the strong framework and color of the house and the backdrop of new black acacia (*A. melanoxylon*) and dodonaea (*D. viscosa* 'Purpurea') hedges.

In the front of the house, a red-flowering trumpet vine (*Distictis buccinatoria*) crawls up the stone chimney, while rambling mounds of Pride of Madeira interspersed with New Zealand flax (*Phormium tenax*) and bronze cordyline assert

themselves against the massive architecture. The overgrown front terrace features woolly thyme (*Thymus pseudolanuginosus*) seeping up between concrete pavers and explosions of red and yellow kangaroo-paws (*Anigozanthos flavidus*). The living room overlooks more Pride of Madeira, which towers above lapping waves of *Senecio mandraliscae*, snow-in-summer (*Cerastium tomentosum*), *Aeonium arboreum* 'Zwartkop', and *Westringia rosmariniformis*. *P. tenax* 'Sundowner', wisteria, and *M. lomariifolia* dominate the entry court, with its bold paving patterns of concrete and brick, while at the farther reaches of the property, native sycamores (*Platanus racemosa*), sugar gums (*Eucalyptus cladocalyx*), and dodonaea shelter a simple, shady pool.

The result is an unabashed sculptural contrivance—a plantsman's garden that delights in calling attention to itself as it energetically knits the house into the larger landscape.

ABOVE: HYBRID KANGAROO-
PAWS, NEW ZEALAND FLAX, AND
SILVER ACACIA BAILEYANA PLAY
AGAINST THE FORMS OF THE HOUSE.
LEFT: NATIVE SYCAMORES
PRESIDE OVER THE POOL.

the
paradise
garden

DREAMING

OF EDEN

Henry Huntington's stunning Rose Garden harbors thousands of varieties.

Artists Tony and Elizabeth Duquette's fantasyland is hidden in a canyon in Beverly Hills.

every garden is someone's version of paradise, a retreat from the noisy, everyday world into an extraordinary realm of natural beauty. Ancient Persians believed that gardens and paradise were synonymous, and conjured up elaborate landscaped parks where the king could walk, relax, and enjoy himself. Chinese imperial gardens featured images of mystical islands, home to immortal beings. When Mohammed spoke to his followers of the gardens of Paradise, he was holding out to them the promise of a happy afterlife. And in Judeo-Christian culture, banishment from the Garden of Eden represented people's forfeiture of blissful eternal life and their doom to an unnatural and conflicted state.

Partly by virtue of their ambition, the gardens included in this chapter qualify as versions of paradise. Although they are not necessarily beautiful, their purpose is to transport visitors to another place—and, in so doing they may challenge our notions of what a garden is. Here, plants tend to be chosen and paired for visual impact rather than horticultural correctness,

and they may share the stage with, or even be upstaged by, elaborate statuary and found objects. Or, in a reversal of the model of garden as nature domesticated, the vegetation might run rampant over everything else—walls, paths, pools— as nature is allowed to reassert its primal claim to the land. In either case, it is the particular, obsessive use of plants which in many ways defines a paradise garden and distinctly sets it apart. Whether spare or luxuriant, reminiscent of stark deserts or of torpid jungles, whether a collection of myriad, uniquely strange specimens or a seemingly endless repetition of the otherwise mundane, paradise gardens are always larger-than-life arenas in which the plants, first and foremost, hold sway.

While contemporary paradise landscapes serve many of the functions of more conventional gardens—extending interior space, providing areas for dining, recreation, and contemplation—they also reflect their creators' fixations and private themes to such an extent that they may be hard for others to comprehend. As might be expected, spiritual elements surface often in paradise gardens. Some are templelike and peaceful while others express individual mystical explorations. Instead of being places simply tailored to the requirements of the people who use them, paradise gardens have an often magical logic of their own, compelling the visitors' attention and guiding them through an experience of the voice and spirit of the garden, on its own terms. While they often contain elements familiar to many garden styles, it is the genius and scale of their combination that makes paradise gardens extraordinary. In many cases it is the most prosaic standby, such as a rose garden planted in rows beside the house, that, when it becomes an obsessive object, seemingly taking on a life of its own, most steals the breath away. It is not necessary that the paradise garden be large, but it must be articulated enough to suggest infinitude, to suggest at once the strivings of its creator and the original, endless garden of nature. The Beverly Hills garden of Tony and Elizabeth Duquette is one example. The modest site has been transformed through careful artifice and whimsy—and a riot of common house plants—into an unutterably exotic landscape. Large or small, a paradise garden is always a transformation of normal space into an effort of transcendence. It is the art of the garden, at its limits, where the garden ceases to be something demarcated, outside of nature, and becomes a kind of inside of its own, an imaginative territory in its own right.

Paradise gardens are just the kind of places that move people to shake their heads and say, "Only in California." After all, few other physical environments would be mild enough to support the relentless crawl of old euphorbias over the face of a house, or welcome an enormous thriving colony of prehistoric cycads. But aside from the hospitality of its weather, California has a history of accepting seekers of paradise, along with their horticultural visions. There's something friendly and tolerant about the state's exotic wildness that has always drawn dreamers to the continent's edge.

PARADISE GARDENS OFTEN EXPRESS LARGER-THAN-LIFE FANTASIES. HUNTINGTON'S DESERT GARDEN CONTAINS MORE THAN 2,500 SPECIMENS OF DRYLAND PLANTS.

PARADISE GARDENS REDEFINE TRADITIONAL IDEAS OF GARDEN BEAUTY. AT LOTUSLAND, EUPHORBIAS GUARD THE ENTRANCE.

Lotusland

Montecito

To those familiar with Homer's *Odyssey*, the name Lotusland suggests a dreamy place where inhabitants live in lazy contentment while nibbling the flowers of forgetfulness. On the other hand, lotus flowers are a powerful, sacred symbol for Buddhists and Hindus. Perhaps the secret of Montecito's Lotusland lies somewhere between the two images. Exotic and strange, this garden served its creator as both a refuge from worldly disappointment and an embodiment of her mystical aspirations.

Ganna Walska bought the thirty-seven acre property in 1941, when, at the age of fifty-eight—a veteran of five marriages and forty years of failure in her chosen career as opera singer—she was turning away from the role of bejeweled socialite and focusing increasingly on her spiritual life. Not one to sit idly by as life passed, she threw herself into the creation of elaborate gardens around her new California home, an undertaking that became her final obsession and one that eventually transformed her into a virtual recluse.

Just down Sycamore Canyon Road from the Old World graces of Casa del Herrero (see page 26), the Walska estate was once the property of the well-known Santa Barbara nurseryman Kinton Stevens. Stevens, who called it Tanglewood, owned the property from 1882 until 1915, and used it for testing tropical and subtropical plants. Indeed, many of the large palms and other major trees at

GANNA WALSKA'S LOTUSLAND WAS CREATED WITH HELP FROM PROFESSIONALS SUCH AS KINTON AND RALPH STEVENS, PETER RIEDEL, LOCKWOOD DE FOREST, AND ISABELLE GREENE.

THE MASSIVE TRUNKS OF CHILEAN WINE PALMS OVERSHADOW THE MOON GARDEN.

Lotusland date back to the Stevens era.

The Gavit family bought the property next and renamed it Cuesta Linda, or "Beautiful Hill." They added a stately Spanish Colonial house designed by architect Reginald Johnson. Later, architect George Washington Smith modified the house and also laid out the perimeter wall and a swimming pool with a tile-roofed bathhouse. Peter Riedel and Paul Thiene created extensive Italianate gardens, including olive trees, lemon *allées*, and a series of formal parterres, and garden designer Lockwood de Forest worked on the entrance court.

De Forest worked later for Walska as well, providing her with drawings for parterres and an aviary. While it is unclear which, if any, of his designs were ever implemented, the notoriously difficult Walska had a much more productive and long-lived rela-

tionship with Ralph Stevens, Kinton's son, who had grown up on the estate.

It was Ralph Stevens who designed the melancholy dream setting of the Blue Garden, with its blue Atlas cedars (*Cedrus atlantica* 'Glauca') and Chilean wine palms (*Jubaea chilensis*) wading like dinosaurs through a sea of blue fescue (*Festuca ovina* 'glauca') and *Seneico mandraliscae*. Stevens also created a mammoth garden clock and an outdoor theater, patterned after one Walska had on the grounds of her chateau in France. (The theater's design was modified and replanted by Santa Barbara landscape artist Isabelle Greene in 1988.)

OPPOSITE: IT IS IN THE GARDEN'S DECORATIVE DETAILS, SUCH AS THE ABALONE-EDGED POOL, THAT WALSKA'S CREATIVE ENERGY RAN RAMPANT.

While Walska radically changed the face of Cuesta Linda's garden structure, she never entirely dismantled it. Among her greatest efforts is the abalone-edged pool decorated with coral islands and giant-clamshell fountains. The pearly blue water and shell decor suggest some wacky version of a tropical paradise, but the water is deceptively shallow, and the banks teem with more than one hundred varieties of South Africa aloes and other desert plants rising out of dry, volcanic gravel.

There are other areas equally stunning for their brooding drama. For instance, the path that curves through the fern garden (designed in 1968 by William Paylen and expanded in 1986) follows a route through a veritable jungle of Australian tree ferns, staghorn ferns, and a host of their feathery relatives. In the bromeliad gardens (also designed by Paylen), ancient coast live oaks (*Quercus agrifolia*) shelter and are all but overrun in places by scores of spiky bromeliads, their cupped centers gleaming with water.

There are also groupings of cacti, euphorbias, and succulents, oddly armored, galactic-shaped debris, and always, in Walska's world, gathered in forbidding numbers as if prepared and willing to defend themselves.

Lotusland was Ganna Walska's greatest stage, her most complete performance. Well before her life's end, she created The Lotusland Foundation to keep it going after her death. Although Walska died in 1984 at the age of one hundred, her gardens opened in 1993 on a limited basis to a public eager to experience her singular vision of paradise.

ONE OF THE MOST STRIKING FEATURES OF LOTUS-LAND IS THE MASSING OF UNUSUAL PLANTS THAT WALSKA ACQUIRED IN THE SAME WAY THAT SHE HAD ONCE BOUGHT CAVIAR AND JEWELS.

Huntington Botanical Gardens

San Marino

ANOTHER GREAT, ONCE-private paradise now open to the public is the Huntington Botanical Gardens of San Marino, former dreaming ground and horticultural laboratory of the wealthy industrialist Henry E. Huntington. In this gently rolling, 207-acre setting, 15 separate gardens feature more than 14,000 plants from around the world, many of them seldom, if ever, seen in California.

The largest landowner in Southern California during his lifetime, Huntington grew up in upstate New York and worked in a hardware store as a child. There he developed the habits of industry and frugality that impressed his uncle, Collis P. Huntington, one of the founders of the Southern Pacific Railroad. In 1892, the younger Huntington moved to San Francisco to become vice-president of his uncle's railroad, and soon afterward moved to Los Angeles to organize his own local Pacific Electric Railway Company. He became involved in the development of electrical power systems, and busied himself buying property. Huntington also played a role in the Owens Valley water scandal, wherein water, ostensibly bound for Los Angeles, was used to irrigate San Fernando Valley farms that investors had bought cheaply and sold at a huge profit—after the water arrived.

In 1900, Huntington's fortunes were augmented by a large inheritance from his uncle, and in 1903, he bought the six-hundred-acre San Marino property, referred to ever afterward as "the ranch." Two

AT ONE TIME, HENRY HUNTINGTON'S JAPANESE GARDEN WAS TENDED BY A JAPANESE FAMILY, WHO ALSO LIVED IN A PAVILION IN THE GARDEN.

THE SCALE AND BLEND OF POWERFUL AND DISPARATE ELEMENTS—PALMS, CAMELLIAS, STATUARY,
CACTUS, AND ROSES—MADE HUNTINGTON'S GARDEN HIS PERSONAL VISION OF PARADISE.

years later, Huntington hired William Hertrich, a German horticulturalist specializing in tropical and exotic plants. For twenty-two years, Hertrich, as impassioned and driven as Huntington himself, traveled to Europe, Mexico, Guatemala, the Carribean, New Zealand, Samoa, and Fiji in search of material for his employer's collections. He assisted in nearly every aspect of the estate's creation and management, even running commercial citrus and avocado operations. After Huntington's death, Hertrich stayed on at the gardens for another two decades, adding new plant collections and expanding existing ones.

In 1913, Huntington married his second wife, Arabella Duval Huntington, his uncle Collis's wid-ow. He spent the rest of his life trying to woo her away from her preferred homes in New York and Paris. For Huntington, California was a heavenly place that could be made even more perfect using the finest obtainable bits and pieces from the rest of the world. The house he built his new wife was a Beaux Arts palace designed by Los Angeles architects Myron Hunt and Elmer Grey, with grand eighteenth-century iron front gates originally made for an English country estate.

Huntington was particular about his plants, authorizing Hertrich to buy up an entire commercial Japanese tea garden operation—landscape, fixtures, buildings, everything—just to obtain authentic, full-grown plant specimens for his Japanese garden.

IN HUNTINGTON'S DESERT GARDEN, AN ENTIRE COLONY OF
GIANT GOLDEN BARREL CACTUS GATHER AROUND MEGALITHIC PASACANA.

Later he hired a Japanese family to tend it and occupy a Japanese-style house there, again for the authenticity they contributed, especially when strolling the grounds in their traditional attire.

The Palm Garden is another of the marvels possible only when enough money and imagination come together. Arrayed in island beds on sloping washes of lawn, ninety species of the shaggy giants toss and clatter in the wind. Even in Southern California, where palm plantings are common, there is something utterly fantastical about whole, dense forests of these elegant, primitive trees. Here, it is possible to examine Mexican, African, and Australian palm species and observe nature's subtle variations on a chosen theme. Chilean wine palms

(*Jubaea chilensis*) have the thickest trunks, while date palms boast magnificent heavy heads. Some palms lean or splay out from their bases; others stand as straight and tall as architectural columns. All present a pleasing contrast between their plain, solid trunks and their wildly sprouting crowns.

In Huntington's most famous landscape, the Desert Garden, 2,500 species of dryland plants coexist in rambling beds edged with volcanic tufa rock originally moved from Santa Cruz in Huntington's private railway cars. Hertrich, not Huntington, was the initial force behind this garden, which, besides the show-stopping cacti, features more than thirty botanical families of plants. Huntington disliked cacti, having backed into one in the Arizona desert,

A BAROQUE FOUNTAIN AND CLASSICAL STATUARY ORNAMENT THE NORTH VISTA.

and had to be persuaded that this particularly in-hospitable scrap of his property might support such an extraordinary collection.

Today, the squat, spiked, snaky congregation Hertrich assembled has reached gargantuan pro-portions. Some of its euphorbias and aloes are the size of huge trees; silvery *Mammillaria compressa* appear to have poured down rocks under the taran-tulalike limbs of *Rathbunia alamosensis*; and serpen-tine *Trichocereus thelegonus* are seemingly caught in the process of heaving up out of the ground. In this garden, and elsewhere throughout the Huntington estate, there is the suggestion of a man concocting for himself an enormous fantasy, collecting images and sensations as much as he was collecting plants.

Earlier than most of his empire-building peers, Huntington saw the potential of Southern Califor-nia and made a fortune from its rapid growth and development. But he was also seized by the romance of the land—by its mountains, its palm trees, its mighty native oaks, its robust and monumental vis-tas. Huntington's San Marino paradise captures the depth of his passion for the place, and his sense that almost anything was possible there, if one only had the vision to conceive it.

OPPOSITE: THE HUNTINGTON BOTANICAL GAR-DENS ALSO CONTAIN HUGE ROSE COLLECTIONS.

Bancroft Garden

Walnut Creek

NEAR SAN FRANCISCO, IN the midst of what was once commercial walnut-growing country, Ruth Bancroft has called forth a sun-drenched desert of incongruities, a place where yuccas, aloes, and succulents gather under tossing Mexican blue palms (*Brahea armata*). Cacti winter in a heated shade house beneath the eaves of a Victorian-style gazebo, while above the dry earth of the garden's winding paths, palo verde (*Parkinsonia aculeata*) fans out like a feather duster. It trails yellow-blooming fronds over some tough characters—*Agave Parryi huachucensis*, euphorbias, and paddle-shaped opuntias—in a fantastic landscape that also harbors 1,000 cultivars of bearded irises.

Bancroft had been gardening for years before she really saw her first succulents. The small handful of aeoniums she collected from someone's backyard in 1954 became the nucleus of a collection that today covers several acres and includes a host of spiny and spidery transplants from the world's deserts. While she still grows impressive numbers of perennials, herbs, roses, and irises in the beds nearest her house, she is most intrigued by the dryland plants. "I love the form and color of their leaves," she says. "Their flowers are just a bonus."

In contrast to the irises and roses, though, her desert specimens must be carefully nursed through the region's cold winters. But the consequence of her efforts is a virtual forest of thriving giants, all of

THESE FLOWERING AGAVES AND OTHER DRYLAND PLANTS COLLECTED BY RUTH BANCROFT MUST BE COAXED THROUGH THE COOL, WET SAN FRANCISCO WINTERS.

A TEDDYBEAR CACTUS SEEMS TO PERCH ON ITS SPIKY NEIGHBORS.

which she acquired at one-gallon size or smaller and many of which have no business living in this environment at all. Under her care, they have not only lived to a ripe old age but have attained magical proportions, transforming her Walnut Creek property into a highly personalized paradise.

Bancroft is modest about her creation, which was formally inaugurated in the early 1970s when her husband suggested she use some of her greenhouse-stored succulents to fill the spot where an old orchard had been removed. The late designer and nurseryman Lester Hawkins from Western Hills Nursery (see page 77) laid out paths and island beds for Bancroft's collection, and also designed the lily pond where the garden's living columns, swords, and paddles jockey for sunlight.

Within Hawkins's framework, Bancroft did the planting, and the garden has evolved ever since under the guidance of her tastes and interest. "I do

it backwards from the way that you're supposed to," she concedes. "I choose what I like and then find a place to fit it in." Contrary to the exotic images of far-flung plant-gathering expeditions that her garden evokes, Bancroft orders specimens from catalogs, doing the traveling only in her mind.

The garden offers a wealth of visual stimulation, a study in contrasts between the gentle and the harsh, the wet and the dry, the welcoming and the forbidding. With plenty of coddling, Bancroft's protégés flourish in a hard place. Their towering yet spindly blooms are images of triumph and, at the same time, reminders of how tentative and fragile existence is, even for those who seem most armed against its dangers.

OPPOSITE: THE DESERT SPECIMENS IN BANCROFT'S GARDEN THRIVE DESPITE THE AREA'S CLIMATE, WHICH IS OFTEN LESS THAN SUITABLE.

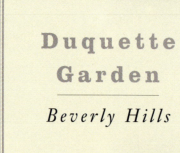

Duquette Garden

Beverly Hills

THE NOTION OF A GARDEN hardly begins to capture the mysterious Shangri-la that artists Tony and Elizabeth Beegle Duquette have been conjuring up for the past forty-four years out of a raw swath of the Beverly Hills canyon. In place of conventional lawns and flower beds, the Duquettes have erected temples, pavilions, and latticed passageways, and then proceeded to turn nature loose on them, creating the effect of a magnificent jungle ruin. Spider plants and ferns dangle from above or sprout from weathered green walls, ivy crawls up gnarled tree trunks, and orchids and bromeliads surge forth around enigmatically smiling stone figures.

The almost palpable spirituality of the place comes in part from the shrinelike enclosures Tony Duquette designed for outdoor dining, entertaining, and garden viewing. The terrace has open, pillared walls curtained with hanging plants, and a latticed roof that provides dappled sun for all-season lunch parties. The dinner pavilion is more heavily shadowed and intimate, and is partly enclosed by antique shutters. Its entrance is guarded by three Chinese statues representing Youth, Middle Age, and Old Age. Nearby stands an ancient-looking pagoda, one of the many that push through the vegetation like relics of antiquity, only to be revealed, on closer look, to be elaborate piles of scrap metal, cement, or even industrial shop lamps welded together for deceptive effect.

Herein lies one of the garden's secrets and plea-

THE DUQUETTE GARDEN IN BEVERLY HILLS IS AN ARTIST'S SHANGRI-LA OF SUSPENDED WALKWAYS AND OUTDOOR LIVING SPACES.

sures: objects in it aren't necessarily what they seem. Tony Duquette is, in fact, a past and present master of the grand illusion. Internationally known for his theatrical and environmental design work, he created the award-winning sets for *Camelot*, as well as the sets and costumes for an impressive number of major films, operas, and ballets. Traveling the world in the course of his career, he and his wife have collected art, artifacts, and decorative bits of architecture from all over Europe and Asia.

Chinese pots, wooden Balinese balls, and carved pediments of Thai houses all participate in the dramatic staging of an imaginary time and place in the Duquette garden. Also involved in the evocation are pieces of scrap metal and cast-off gangplanks acquired at a naval auction; a battered balustrade from Falcon's Lair, the one-time home of movie

LEFT: MANY OF THE ORNAMENTS IN THE DUQUETTE GARDEN ARE MADE OF SCRAP OR INEXPENSIVE MATERIALS. ABOVE: THE LARGE TERRACE, WITH ITS LATTICED ROOF, IS PERFECT FOR ENTERTAINING IN SOUTHERN CALIFORNIA'S YEAR-ROUND MILD CLIMATE.

star Rudolph Valentino; and a pair of eighteenth-century garden chairs designed by William Kent. With a mixed sense of fun and visionary purpose, Duquette folds together trash and treasures into double-take compositions. Two iridescent obelisks behind the priceless Kent chairs turn out to be bits of abalone shell glued to metal frames. A "carved jade" wall panel is actually perforated, painted plastic, while a magical glass that captures a tiny, funhouse garden in its sphere is a common lawn ornament from Mexico.

Like the pagodas and the bridges that link up various garden areas and exotic outbuildings, the plants in this landscape function more as sculptural elements than as individual stage-grabbing specimens. Of primary interest are their color and shape; thus, a dense canopy of pines and eucalyptus rustles overhead, and a giant copa d'oro vine (*Solandra maxima*) turns an airy bridge into a tunnel. In the distance, between the peaks of the two buildings, the tall flower spikes of century plants (*Agave americana*) rise like smoke plumes on a hillside.

The modest, faintly pink house, built in 1949, is now half-smothered in vegetation and layers of sculpture. Wandering in the garden, which evolved, Tony Duquette says, "like a picture, without a plan," it is easy to forget there's a house there at all. This is especially true at night, when the entire fanciful world is seen by candlelight that jumps and dances in the pagoda windows, and every stairway appears to lead upward to the gates of eternity.

BITS OF PLASTIC, PRICELESS WILLIAM KENT CHAIRS, CARVED THAI PEDIMENTS, AND JUNKED NAVAL EQUIPMENT ALL ADD TO WHAT TONY DUQUETTE CALLS "A LIVING COROMANDEL, A SIXTEENTH-CENTURY CHINESE SCREEN FULL OF PAGODAS, BRIDGES, AND TREES."

Newton Garden

St. Helena

FOR NAPA VALLEY'S PETER and Su Hua Newton, the concept of Eden runs the gamut from terraced grape arbors and formal parterres to minimalist Zen landscapes and melancholy screens of weeping trees. The road winding up through their 560-acre property cuts across picturesque vineyards, past an English perennial garden, banks of gardenias, and the extraordinary sight of three tiers of blue and purple tree wisteria (*W. sinensis*) flowing in rippling, parallel formation along the curves of a hill. Eleven different gardens in all unfold along the dips and rises of their Spring Mountain landscape, which is also the site of Newton Vineyard, Peter Newton's Napa Valley winery, founded in 1978.

Newton's dream for this landscape began with a clean slate, with five raw acres he literally carved off the top of a mountain and terraced to overlook the flowing order of his vineyards and the wilder tumble of the Mayacamas range in the distance. His challenge, while integrating his gardens into these surroundings, was to create intimate spaces despite the overwhelming splendor of the view. Slices of mountains, vineyard, and sky appear in the garden rooms through trailing fingers of vines, or beside heaped, dripping rose arbors, or through screens of trees spreading, weeping, rising in tall, straight spires or playful corkscrews.

Newton's careful pairing of color and texture links the garden's disparate tableaux. The bristly

PETER AND SU HUA NEWTON'S PARADISE ENCOMPASSES VINEYARDS, MEADOWS, AND PLAYFUL FORMAL GARDENS.

THE NEWTON GARDEN
DISPLAYS A MASTERFUL
INTERPLAY OF RIGID AND
FLOWING GEOMETRIES
ADAPTED TO ITS
MAGNIFICENT SITE.

variations among white roses, purple bush germander (*Teucrium fruticans*), and silver santolina are packed into the cross-hatchings of a box hedge as neatly as candy into a candy box. In other areas, hot hues of Delbar's orange roses are piled on a pergola while icy cobalt East Friesland salvia electrifies the weeping garden beneath pale, unraveling skeins of Atlas cedar (*Cedrus atlantica*). A rare prostrate Cedar-of-Lebanon (*C. libani*) grows like a fountain among golden deodars (*C. Deodara*) and golden Atlas cedars (*C. atlantica*) around the Zen landscape, and the Italian cypresses (*Cupressus sempervirens*) that rise on the lower periphery of the croquet lawn are a golden tipped cultivar from Australia. Even the common plants are treated in novel ways, unexpectedly sheared, grafted, and massed to produce otherworldly effects. Newton seems to be calling attention throughout to the staggering plenitude and potential of both nature and the imagination.

LEFT: A WEEPING BLUE ATLAS CEDAR TUMBLES FROM A PERGOLA ABOVE STONE PATHS AND FORMAL PARTERRES DOMINATED BY COBALT-BLUE SALVIA FRIESLANDII. ABOVE: AN ANTIQUE BASIN STANDS IN THE VAST ROSE GARDEN.

the
contemporary
garden

A DIALOGUE WITH
MODERN ARCHITECTURE

THE BEEBE-YUDELL GARDEN
OVERFLOWS WITH WINTER-
BLOOMING ROSES.

THE SCHNABEL GARDEN IN BRENTWOOD
IS A COLORFUL TAPESTRY WOVEN OF
DROUGHT-TOLERANT TREES AND PERENNIALS.

N CALIFORNIA, AS IN THE rest of the world, the notion of the garden constantly changes. Over the past two centuries the western garden has functioned in turn as an agrarian center and refuge from the wild frontier, a public display of wealth and status, a piece of idealized or romanticized nature, a retreat from an increasingly mechanized world, and a private family playground.

The reasons for these shifts range from the practical to the philosophical. California has come a long way from its early hardscrabble days, but even for those who enjoy year-round, modern outdoor living, leisure time increases or diminishes during certain periods, and time spent in the garden rises or falls accordingly. Californians have often felt flush and entitled to create a paradise of tropical flamboyance in the semiarid portions of the state, but at other times they have been impelled—by drought, overdevelopment, and diminishing resources—toward more ecologically responsible, appropriate designs. In California, the availability of water fluctuates as much as the economic picture.

Of course, dominant landscape trends, like architectural styles, are never universally adopted. As the previous chapters show, great California gardens are regularly designed in some variation of the mission style; or in the vocabulary of Italianate or French formal gardens; or along the relaxed, naturalistic lines of cottage plots. Californians are nothing if not tolerant of one another's eclectic tastes.

Although trends in garden design vary, twentieth-century landscape architects have on the whole radically rethought the way outdoor spaces are shaped and used. Placing less effort on trying to wrestle nature into classical designs, they have increasingly moved away from the idea of gardens as self-contained creations that bear little relation to their natural surrounds. In the prosperous years that followed World War II, for example, designers such as Garrett Eckbo and Thomas Church relinquished the Beaux Arts insistence on ideal forms. Harvard-trained, both moved west to practice, and they took as their starting point client needs and family-oriented usage of private landscape. Their designs were asymmetrical and free-flowing, drawing their inspiration from such diverse sources as modern abstract art and Japanese gardens. Patios, barbecues, swimming pools, and fresh-air dining spots abounded in open, low-maintenance landscapes, as uncluttered and easy to use as a fifties-style all-electric kitchen.

Other landscape architects took the simplicity of modern design to a minimalist extreme, attempting to eliminate all but the merest suggestions of an outdoor framework that might serve the traditional function of a usable garden. By and large, these landscape architects and their successors rejected overtly historical references in favor of more universally understood imagery. And in recent years, preservation issues and eco-consciousness have figured as largely in landscape design as did the modernist ideology of the midcentury. Designers and their clients have become far more aware of the garden as part of a natural and stylistic contin-

uum that extends beyond the specific site to include the locality and the region. In balancing appropriate plant selection with aesthetic and design considerations, contemporary gardens have achieved an unprecedented fit with their surroundings.

Because most of the gardens in this chapter were created either by garden designers or by horticulturally oriented landscape architects, they don't participate directly in landscape architecture's modern spatial debate; but they grow out of it and draw on it. These designs, for the most part, are asymmetrical rather than axial and are conceived as appropriate partners to contemporary architecture. The use of plants tends to be contrived, abstract, and painterly rather than naturalistic.

Still, the goal remains the same: to seduce the eye with a profusion of organic shapes, forms, and colors and to draw people outside to smell the flowers, hear the leaves rustle, and experience the profound connection between the built and the natural worlds. It is this experience, finally, that is the *raison d'être* for a garden.

Isabelle Greene's Valentine garden is a contemporary interpretation of the Mediterranean terraced landscape.

Cypress and eucalyptus cast long shadows in a quiet corner of the Martin garden.

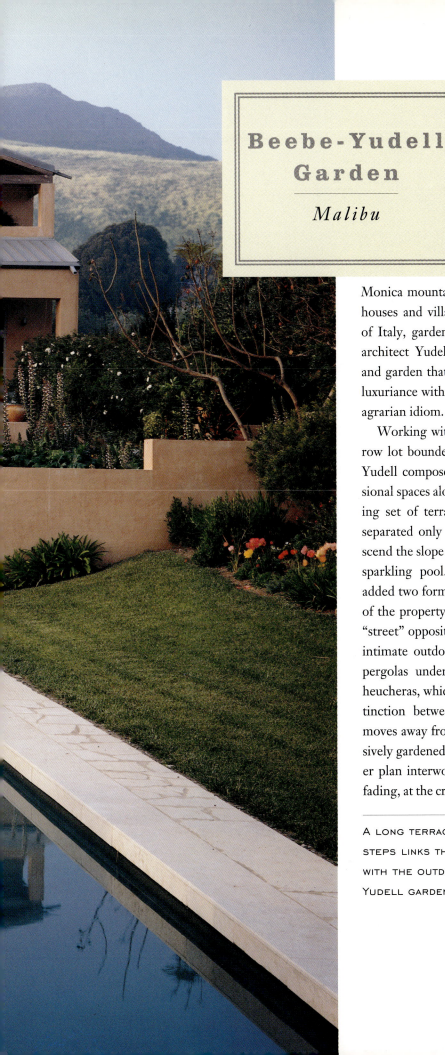

Beebe-Yudell Garden

Malibu

WITH A BREATHTAKING view of the Pacific sprawled out before it to the south, the Malibu refuge of Buzz Yudell and Tina Beebe rests like a small jewel on the breast of the western Santa Monica mountains. Inspired by the Tuscan farmhouses and villas they had studied on their tours of Italy, garden designer and colorist Beebe and architect Yudell designed a very personal house and garden that deftly marry a sense of California luxuriance with the elegance of the Mediterranean agrarian idiom.

Working within the constraints of a long, narrow lot bounded to the west by a seasonal creek, Yudell composed the house as a series of processional spaces along a single axis formed by a matching set of terraced "streets"—inside and outside separated only by French doors—that gently descend the slope of the property, arriving finally at a sparkling pool. To this framework Beebe first added two formal orchards: olives at the south end of the property and citrus at the north. Along the "street" opposite the house, she created a series of intimate outdoor rooms formed by rose-covered pergolas underplanted with poppies, irises, and heucheras, which both accentuate and blur the distinction between interior and exterior. As one moves away from the house, the geometric, intensively gardened spaces gradually give way to a looser plan interwoven with meandering paths finally fading, at the creek's edge, into a wild tumble of tall

A LONG TERRACED "STREET" OF DESCENDING STEPS LINKS THE OPEN ROOMS OF THE HOUSE WITH THE OUTDOOR ROOMS OF THE BEEBE-YUDELL GARDEN.

THE GARDEN'S BURGEONING PLANTS SEEM TO BE CLAMORING TOWARD THE HOUSE.

native chaparral plants such as *Ceanothus* 'Concha', fremontodendron, and toyon (*Heteromeles arbutifolia*).

Once a tomato farm that bore three harvests each year (the lot's narrow shape had in fact been determined by the length that one could conveniently plow), the site is rich with alluvial soil that sustains a cornucopia of edible delights. In addition to being beautiful, the fecund garden is also true to the agrarian roots of Mediterranean style. Of her former truck farm, Beebe says, "I like the idea of going out to the garden to get dinner." Although she began by designating a defined kitchen garden, she soon found that, to keep the ravenous resident go-

phers guessing, the vegetables were better intermingled with the rest of the garden, tucked into odd places among her perennials. Now, the profusion is astounding, as the entire garden—like the *fraises des bois* that have jumped out of their confining pots and run rampant in the cracks between the patio paving stones, where the cool root run is more to their liking—seems to be escaping its bounds.

OPPOSITE: ABOVE THE HOUSE, A GRAY-GREEN ALLÉE OF EDIBLE PINEAPPLE GUAVAS REPEATS THE NOTE OF THE OLIVE ORCHARD AT THE PROPERTY'S SOUTHERN END.

ABOVE: IRISES AND ECHEVERIAS MAKE
THEMSELVES AT HOME. RIGHT: THE INTIMATE
UPPER PATIO ECHOES THE SERENITY OF THE
EARLY MISSION COURTYARDS.

Schnabel Garden

Brentwood

ONE OF THE PURPOSES OF landscape design is to knit together the disparate elements of a place, to link a home and its setting in a unified stage for living. Traditionally, a garden has also provided areas for private contemplation apart from the busy social and functional centers of the home. Certain ancient cultures—the Greeks, the Romans, and the Chinese—took the garden retreat a step further, constructing scholars' pavilions in the landscape for writing and study. The Schnabel house and garden in Brentwood, a collaborative project by architect Frank Gehry, owner Maria Schnabel, and me draws on this classical model. The result is a contemporary deconstruction of traditional domestic space into a series of singular pavilions connected with gardens.

Although the house is secluded from the street by a high white wall, the bold volumes of its outbuildings are visible against the sky. They will eventually be screened by black acacias and olive trees, but in the meantime, such forceful forms called for a simple yet equally assertive front planting. The combination of smoke-blue century plants (*Agave americana*) set in a blue-green sea of *Seneico mandraliscae* is used here as it was in old Montecito estate gardens, where it would form a border between the street and the private space within.

Just inside the gates, there's a different feeling altogether from the coolness of the front, with a mix of flashy colors and diverse textures in a long

ARCHITECT FRANK GEHRY, GARDEN DESIGNER NANCY POWER, AND OWNER MARIA SCHNABEL COLLABORATED ON THIS CONTEMPORARY HOUSE AND GARDEN IN BRENTWOOD.

AN OLIVE ORCHARD IS UNDERPLANTED WITH GRAY GRASSES,
SPARAXIS, AND ORANGE CALIFORNIA POPPIES.

Mediterranean border visible from the main living pavilion, the study pavilion, and the balcony off the garage. Strap-leafed plants are profuse here, and preeminent among them are a number of bronze flaxes, cordylines, and leafy bird-of-paradise. Tall *Beschorneria yuccoides*, the shaggy lavender of statice, the hunched black plum of *Aeonium arboreum* 'Zwartkop', *S. mandraliscae*, and the jelly palm *Butia capitata* mix beautifully with a stand of giant, flame-red Brazilian cannas (*Canna* x *generalis*).

Across the flagstone entry path from the border, the silver grays of an olive grove blend an under-

planting of gray grass from Morocco, orange California poppies, and sparaxis. Just as the Romans always imbued their town gardens with a country flavor, this Mediterranean-style grove adds a soft agrarian feel to the space, a fitting complement to a world of strong, uncompromising forms.

OPPOSITE, ABOVE: A BORDER OF AGAVES AND SENECIO LOOKS DROP-DEAD MODERN.
OPPOSITE, BELOW: THIS BORDER WAS INSPIRED BY A PHOTO FOUND IN WINIFRED STARR DOBYN'S 1931 BOOK CALIFORNIA GARDENS.

Valentine Garden

Montecito

THE VALENTINE GARDEN is, perhaps, the most dramatic and well-known work of landscape architect Isabelle Greene. Here she transformed a precipitous slope in the Santa Ynez foothills into shallow, irregular terraces, creating flat planes to hold a living, abstract painting. To see the garden up close—to enter its small Zen courtyard and move alongside its slate-edged pool and symbolic stone stream, to descend a series of steps through its three elaborately crazy-quilted tiers—is to experience all the sensual gratifications of creative planting and finely shaped space. But the real view, the one that taps into everyone's imagination, is the one from above. From the balcony of a spare, sculptural house designed for Carol Valentine by architect Paul Gray, the land below appears swept and stroked by subtle color fields, washed with rock rivers, magically flattened and boldly readable—like the aerial views of farm fields that Greene points to as an inspiration for the design.

Mass planting contributes to her vivid effects: snow-in-summer (*Cerastium tomentosum*) pools and swirls against a lava flow of *Seneico mandraliscae*, which is interrupted here and there by spiny agaves. A nubby, rust-colored rug of pork and beans (*Sedum x rubrotinctum*) seeps between the fleshy, clamoring fingers of medicinal aloes and the silver swords of our-Lord's-candle (*Yucca whipplei*). Against the spindly poles of a pergola, featherbeds of evergreen candytuft (*Iberis sempervirens*) and dusty-miller

ISABELLE GREENE COMBINED HER OUTSTANDING KNOWLEDGE OF PLANTS WITH HER ARCHITECTURAL USE OF STONE AND CAST CONCRETE TO DESIGN THIS MASTERFUL CONTEMPORARY GARDEN.

THE VALENTINE GARDEN WAS INSPIRED BY AERIAL VIEWS OF AGRICULTURAL FIELDS.

(*Centaurea cineraria*) show up plumply, while nearby, several *Agave victoriae-reginae* form a party of neat restraint below a messy heap of fountain grass. Much of Greene's palette is drought tolerant, a necessity for the property—which came with only a meager water allotment—and a fringe benefit of her partiality for silver-thread plantings.

Greene's work tends to blend an affection for nature with an appreciation of abstract forms, a mix that reflects her combined early training as a botanist and an artist. Paul Gray designed the house in a style that recalls North African village structures and pared-down pueblos. Greene then surrounded it with southwestern-flavored elements—gray-green foliage set against a warmth of beige gravel. With a softening brush stroke of brilliant red bougainvillea, she incorporated the home's white walls into the garden, and she further naturalized their stark, modern planes with an espaliered fig tree underplanted with crenallated lavender.

The Zen garden is a compressed courtyard hemmed in by walls and trees, and alive with the real and symbolic splash of water. From the irregular pool—which looks as if it has been chipped and gouged from flinty ground—a wash of broken slate flows off toward the back of the house and downhill across the patchwork terraces. The low, asymmetrical terrace walls are fashioned of colored cast concrete. Within the irregular confines of these walls are succulents, perennials, and an array of annuals side by side in a jostling mosaic. From the balcony, the view can appear, by turns, as an exotic tapestry or a collision of continents—the fragments of a picture that the eye perceives as a startling whole.

OPPOSITE: GREENE'S DESIGN IS A MODERN INTERPRETATION OF THE GARDEN AS A REFUGE FROM THE WILD FRONTIER.

Stringfellow Garden

Los Angeles

WHEN SUSAN STRINGFELLOW set out to add on to her 1920s John Byers–designed Spanish Colonial Revival house, she knew from the start that the garden would become a crucial element in the design process. The striking modern addition, designed by Los Angeles architects Paul Lubowicki and Susan Lanier, is a subtle composition of textured, rectilinear volumes that articulate and extend the lines of the original structure into the rear garden. Working closely with Stringfellow, I was given what is perhaps the ultimate challenge for any garden designer: creating a garden space that preserves the integrity and feel of the existing landscape elements while responding to the contemporary vocabulary of strong new architecture.

Just as Stringfellow wanted the addition, through careful repetition of materials and details, to form a seamless link between old and new, she had always thought of the house and garden as a single, harmonious composition, with little distinction between inside and outside. To weave the two elements together, we first placed a long water-lily pool at the corner of the master bedroom, slightly off the central axis of the house, where its reflection can be seen from almost every room. Taking advantage of the dining room's glass doors, a stone terrace extends the living space outside before dissolving into a loose, planted stone pathway that encircles a magnificent old pomegranate tree (*Punica granatum*). At the base of the terrace's patterned concrete wall, a sculptural stream of brown river

NANCY POWER DESIGNED GRANITE PATHS THAT
MEANDER THROUGH A FIELD OF LAVENDER BESIDE
SUSAN STRINGFELLOW'S HOUSE.

THE DINING ROOM OPENS ONTO A TERRACE SHADED BY A GNARLED POMEGRANATE TREE.

rock flows between the house and the spill basin of the lily pool.

To soften the hard lines of the building, diagonal paths of decomposed granite are set into a sea of billowing lavender (*Lavandula multifida*) extending out to a sunny, Mediterranean border of purple-flowering Pride of Madeira (*Echium fastuosum*), *Geranium incanum*, *Aster* x *frikartii*, yellow Jerusalem sage (*Phlomis fruticosa*), white Matilija poppies (*Romneya coulteri*), and chartreuse *Euphorbia characias* 'wulfennii'. Taking a cue from the strong presence of existing trees—a towering eucalyptus and a purple-flowering jacaranda—four more jacarandas preside over a small Buffalo-grass meadow edged with bright, turquoise-berried *Dianella tasmanica*. Climbing roses spread over the garage and wall at the rear, providing year-round color.

In the front garden we chose to retain the simple, elegant feel of the original lines and plantings. Using old, weathered bricks, we extended what had once been a narrow driveway to link the rear garden with the intimate entry courtyard. Two espaliered Australian tea trees (*Leptospermum laevigatum*) adorn a new courtyard wall, and more plants were added to bolster the existing clumps of orange, wandlike orchids (*Epidendrum ibaguense*) and the succulent green rosettes of *Aeonium pseudotabuliforme*. To match the color and texture of the single deodar (*Cedrus deodara*) that dominates the front garden, I added a screen of *Juniperus chinensis* 'Ro-

OPPOSITE: AGAVE AMERICANA AND EUPHORBIA CHARACIAS 'WULFENII' ARE IN STRIKING CONTRAST IN THE STRINGFELLOW GARDEN.

busta Green', a classic but now rarely seen deep green conifer that also grows at my nearby 1920s house. To replace what had been dirt we added a decomposed granite parking court, edged with bird-of-paradise (*Strelitzia reginae*) and a swath of *Agave americana* set in *Senecio mandraliscae* and more euphorbias. A clump of yuccas, almost certainly left over from the house's original landscaping, completes the picture—a living example of continuity between classic and modern, old and new.

ABOVE AND RIGHT: DELICATE EPIDENDRUM ORCHIDS LINE THE ORIGINAL ENTRY PATIO.

OPPOSITE: SEEN FROM THE MASTER BEDROOM, THE WATER LILY TANK HIDES IN THE LAVENDER.

COLLABORATING OVER a period of three years with architect Richard Martin on his Brentwood garden was an experience of constant challenge, discovery, and surprise. The steep, brush-covered site, perched high on a hillside above Los Angeles with sweeping views of the mountains and the Pacific, presented us with enormous opportunities but few obvious solutions. Because of its scale, at times extreme topography, and exposure to withering canyon winds, an easy, traditional garden was out of the question. As Martin says, "The garden evolved over time; it was intuition more than anything else. We did it on the ground, tramping around the site, laying out paths, and choosing plant combinations by holding fistfuls of one thing up against another."

Because we worked slowly and carefully, listening to what the site had to say, the garden soon took on a wonderful and multifaceted shape. We began by moving in a gnarled coast live oak (*Quercus agrifolia*) that would become the center of the entry courtyard, and by planting a perimeter screen of fast-growing black acacias (*A. melanoxylon*) underplanted with purple hop bushes (*Dodonaea viscosa* 'Purpurea'). The next step was creating destinations and surprises in the garden; and as a way to discover them, laying out a network of decomposed granite paths following the contours of the land. Because of its size, it is not possible to see the entire garden at once, instead one is required to make sev-

NANCY POWER AND RICHARD MARTIN DESIGNED THIS HILLSIDE GARDEN, WHICH SEEMS TO UNDULATE WITH THE TERRAIN.

eral passes, on differing routes, to get a complete sense of its varying moods.

Planting one area at a time, we found that large, dramatic sweeps of strong, contrasting materials were not only visually effective against the undulations of the hillside but also eased the task of gardening on so large a site by making the weeds quickly identifiable! The complex color that Martin had painted his newly completed house—a pale Roman red with coral and raspberry undertones— dictated the garden's palette. Although the dominant flower color in the garden is the purple of jacarandas, *Ceanothus* 'Concha', *Echium fastuosum*,

LEFT AND BELOW: THE ALMOST-HUMAN FORMS OF THE ALOES, AGAVES, AND BLUE GUM TREES SET THE MOOD IN THE MOON GARDEN.

AN ALOE BAINESII TREE AND WINTER-DORMANT WATER LILIES GRACE THE ENTRY COURT.

and four different varieties of lavender, the plantings range across a rich, distinct color band from black and bronze to silver-gray, yellow, chartreuse, and a bit of white, with myriad coral-red hues in between.

We visited nurseries in search of plants that we liked, whether common or rare, native or exotic, and placed them in the garden in sometimes offbeat combinations. Blue *Iris* x *germanica* 'Breakers' and *Convolvulus mauritanicus* nestle with spiky *Agave desmettiana*. Night-blooming *Cereus* cactus sprout from feathery, silver *Artemisia* 'Powis Castle'. The fiery flower spikes of jumbled aloes color the shade beneath oaks and chalky-blue *Eucalyptus globulus*, while the otherworldly, tangled structure of *Corokia cotoneaster* contrasts with succulent native dudleyas and *Agave attenuata*. When arranging progressions and groupings of plants, we often found ourselves more interested in the color and texture of their foliage than in their flowers. Instead of arranging single specimens together—as one might, for example, in a small cottage garden—we found that the garden responded well to bold moves, and so we grouped plants according to their subtle gradations of color, shape, and mass.

From any point in the garden, the effect is one of definite layering, at once organic because of the site's topography and also abstract, like a colorist painting. In the grass meadow that we designed with help from friend, nurseryman, and garden designer John Greenlee, a wave of alternating stripes of fall-colored tall grasses appears to break over a playing field of gray-green Buffalo-grass (*Buchloe dactyloides*). When one stands at the bottom of the property looking up toward the house, one sees first the periwinkle-blue flags of the irises against the spikes of agaves, then a tapestry of reds—pink proteas (*P. neriifolia* 'Pink Ice'), crimson-leaved *Leucodendron* 'Safari Sunset', bronze flax, and red fountain grass—which fades into a field of lavender climbing up the hill beneath blue palms (*Butia capitata*) and, finally, an orchard of silver olive trees.

BELOW: Waves of proteas, grasses, lavender, and olives wrap the hillside.
OVERLEAF: The steel fountain's destination amid palms and lavender; the secluded moon garden.

TISCH GARDEN

Acacia baileyana 'purpurea'
A. melanoxylon
A. pendula
Aeonium arboreum 'Zwartkop'
Ajuga reptans
Aloe barbadensis
A. saponaria
A. striata
Anigozanthos flavidus
Armeria maritima 'alba'
Billbergia nutans
Brugmansia versicolor
Cerastium tomentosum
Clematis armandii
Clivia minata
Cordyline australis
    'atropurpurea'
Crassula falcata
Dierama pulcherrimum
Disticts buccinatoria
D. x riversii
Dodonaea viscosa 'Purpurea'
Echeveria x imbricata
Echium fastuosum
Elaeagnus pungens
Eryngium planum
Eucalyptus cladocalyx
Helichrysum petiolatum
    'Limelight'
Helleborus corsicus
Heuchera 'Palace Purple'
Iris x germanica
Kalanchoe tomentosa
Lamium maculatum
Lavandula angustifolia
Leonotis menthifolia
Liriope muscari
Lonicera hildebrandiana
Lotus berthelottii
Lychnis coronaria
Lycianthus ratonnei
Mahonia lomariifolia
Manfreda variegata
Melianthus major
Muehlenbeckia axillaris
Nandina domestica
Nerium oleander
Ophiopogon planiscapus
    'Nigresceus'

Parthenocissus quinquefolia
Passiflora jamesonii
Phormium tenax
P. tenax 'atropurpureum'
Platanus racemosa
Romneya coulteri
Rosmarinus officinalis
Senecio mandraliscae
Solandra maxima
Sparaxis tricolor
Stachys byzantina
Ternstroemia gymnanthera
Teucrium fruticans
Thymus pseudolanuginosus
T. serpyllum
Viola labradorica
Westringia rosmariniformis

BEEBE-YUDELL GARDEN

Roses (Climbers)
Alchymist
Belle of Portugal
Brownell's Pink Pillar
Cécile Brunner
Gloire de Dijon
Lady Banks
Meg
Mme. Alfred Carrière
Mme. Grégoire Staechelin
Mrs. Sam McGreedy
New Dawn
Soleil d'Or
Souvenir de la Malmaison

Roses (Shrub)
Cornelia
Mutabilis
Nymphenburg
Robbie Burns
Sally Holmes
Shropshire Lass
Susan Louise

Rose Fence
Albertine
Complicata
Francois Juranville
Frühlingsmorgen
Golden Wings
Léontine Gervais

Mermaid
Mme. Pierre Oger
Mme. Victor Verdier
Nevada
Paul's Himalyan Musk
Rosa alba 'Semi Plena'
R. bracteata
R. swegenzowii
Sally Holmes
Shot Silk
Yolande d'Aragon

Rose Border
Anna Pavlova
Apricot Nectar
Baroness Rothchild
Buff Beauty
Catherine Mermat
Celsiana
Comte de Chambord
Cuisse de Nymphe
Duet
Fantin-Latour
Félicité Parmentier
Fortune's Five Color
Frau Dagmar Hastrup
Golden Wings
Gruss an Aachen
Helen Traubel
Hume's Blush
Iceberg
Königin von Dänemark
La Marne
Lady Hillingdon
Maitland White
Marbree
Marquise Bocella
Medallion
Mme. Hardy
Mrs. Oakley Fisher
Mrs. R. D. Charmian Crawford
Paul's Early Blush
Peace
Penelope
Rosa rugosa 'Rubra'
Rosa Sancta
Rose de Provence
Safrano
Summer Wind
Tiffany
Yves Piaget

Roses (English)
Abraham Darby
Ambridge Rose
Belle Story
Bredon
Canterbury
Charles Rennie Mackintosh
Cottage Rose
Cymbeline
Emanuel
English Garden
Ellen
Gertrude Jekyll
Graham Thomas
Heritage
Jacquenetta
Jane Austin
Kathryn Morley
L. D. Braithwaite
Lilian Austin
Lucetta
Mary Rose
Mary Webb
Peach Blossom
Perdita
Pretty Jessica
Proud Titania
Sir Walter Raleigh
St. Cecilia
Sweet Juliet
Tamora
The Prioress
The Yeoman
Wenlock
Wife of Bath
Winchester Cathedral

Rose Border Understories
Alchemilla mollis
Anemone japonica 'Sylvestris'
Campanula sp.
Convolvulus mauritanicus
Dorycnium hirsutum
Erodium petalum 'Crispum'
Fragaria vesca
Geranium albanum
G. 'Baxton's Blue'
G. 'Johnson's Blue'
G. Riversleaianum 'Mavis Simpson'
G. sanguineum
G. subcaulescens 'Russel Pritchard'
Ipheion uniflorum 'Wisley Blue'

Iris x germanica
I. pallida 'Orris'
Linum perenne
Lychnis Coronaria 'Alba'
Myosotis sp.
Narcissus 'Thalia'
Oxypetalum caeruleum 'Tweedia'
Papaver rhoeas, Papaver
    somniferum, Papaver 'Kobe
    Salmon', Papaver flanders
Salvia chamaedrys
Scabiosa 'Villa Emo'
Stachys lanata
Teucrium fruticans
Viola odorata

Bird Border
Cistus sp.
Convolvulus cneorum
Euphorbia rigida
E. wulfenii
E. wulfenii 'Marina'
Grevillea 'Victoria'
Helianthemum nummularium
Helichrysum petiolatum
    'Limelight'
Leptospermum laevigatum
    'Reevesii'
Lobelia laxiflora
Macleaya microcarpa
Melianthus major
Perovskia atriplicifolia
Rhamnus californica 'Eve Case'
Salvia discolor
S. rutilans
Sedum spectabile
Silene maritima
Yucca recurvifolia

Mediterranean Border
Arbutus 'Marina'
Argemone sp.
Brahea armata
Cistus salviifolius
C. skanbergii
Correa pulchella
Diplacus longiflorus
Eriogonum giganteum
Euphorbia rigida
Galvezia speciosa
Grevillea 'Victoria'
Helianthemum nummularium

Hesperaloe parviflora
Iochroma cyaneum
Iris Douglasiana
Penstemon 'Midnight'
Perovskia atriplicifolia
Rhagodia spinescens deltoides
Salvia chamaedrys
S. 'Costa Rican Blue'
S. discolor
S. gesneriflora 'Tequila'
S. greggii 'Salmon'
S. guaranitica
S. 'Indigo Spires'
S. leucantha 'Midnight'
S. muelleri
S. patens
S. rutilans
S. splendens
S. uliginosa
S. viridis
Sisyrinchium bellum
Sphaeralcea munroana
Verbascum olympicum
Verbena bonariensis
Zauschneria californica

Arroyo Edge
Arbutus unedo
Ceanothus 'Concha'
C. griseus horizontalis
C. 'herstiorum'
C. 'Ray Hartman'
Dendromecon harfordii
Echium fastuosum
Fremontodendron 'San Gabriel'
Heteromeles arbutifolia
Quercus agrifolia
Romneya coulteri

Hedges
Arbutus unedo
Grevillea 'Victoria'
Laurus nobilis
Rosa 'Iceberg'
Rosmarinus officinalis
    'Tuscan Blue'

Jacaranda Border
Agapanthus africanus
Brodiaea laxa (Triteleia laxa)
Campanula glomerata 'Alba'
C. persicifolia

C. rapunculoides
Carpenteria californica
Clerodendrum ugandeuse
Datura suaveolens
Duranta repens
Gladiolus 'Acidantherus'
Lonicera hildebrandiana
Moraea iridiodes 'Lemon Drop'
Platycodon grandiflorus
Rosa 'Mermaid'
Verbascum chaixii

Pots
Agave attenuata
A. desmettiana
Aloe vera
Bulbine sp.
Citrus sinensis (dwarf)
Dudleya pulverulenta
Echeveria x imbricata
Opuntia Ficus-indica
O. robusta
Pelargonium spp.: fragrans;
    odorantissimum; graveolens;
    crispum; tomentosum
Trichocereus pachanoi

Echium fastuosum
Eschscholzia californica
Eucalyptus citriodora
E. ficifolia
Iris x germanica
Jacaranda mimosifolia
Lavandula multifida
Leptospermum scoparium
    'Ruby Glow'
Limonium perezii
Lonicera halliana
Melaleuca nesophylla
Melianthus major
Nerium oleander
Olea europaea
Phormium tenax
P. tenax 'atropurpureum'
Pittosporum crassifolium
Quercus agrifolia
Romneya coulteri
Rosmarinus officinalis
    'Tuscan Blue'
Salvia leucantha
Senecio mandraliscae
Sparaxis tricolor
Tibouchina urvilleana

Kalanchoe sieboldii
Lantana 'Radiation'
Lavandula angustifolia
Lewisia sp.
Morus pendula
Parthenocissus tricuspidata
Phormium tenax
    'Rubrum Dwarf'
Romneya coulteri
Rosa 'Belle of Portugal'
R. 'Cecil Brunner'
R. rugosa
Salvia sp.
Sedum brevifolium
S. x rubrotinctum
Sempervivum arachnoideum
S. montanum 'braunii'
Senecio haworthii
S. mandraliscae
S. serpens
S. Vira-vira
Stachys byzantina
Thymus serpyllum lanuginosus
Vitex agnus-castus
Westringia rosmariniformis
Yucca whipplei

SCHNABEL GARDEN
Acacia melanoxylon
Acanthus mollis
Aeonium arboreum 'Zwartkop'
Agapanthus africanus
Agave americana
A. attenuata
Aloe arborescens
Anigozanthos flavidus
Beschorneria yuccoides
Bougainvillea 'Orange King'
B. 'California Gold'
Brahea armata
Brugmansia versicolor
Butia capitata
Canna sp.
Carissa macrocarpa 'tuttlei'
Ceanothus 'Ray Hartmann'
Cordyline australis
    'autropurpurea'
Dietes iridiodes
Dodonaea viscosa 'Purpurea'
Doryanthes palmeri
Dracaena draco
Echeveria elegans

VALENTINE GARDEN
Aeonium urbicum
Agave celsii
A. potatorum
A. sisalana
A. victoriae-reginae
Aloe barbadensis
A. wickensii
Calocephalus brownii
Centaurea cineraria
Cerastium tomentosum
Cotyledon macrantha
C. orbiculata
Crassula arborescens
Crassula falcata
Dasylirion wheeleri
Doryanthes palmeri
Dudleya brittonii
Echeveria setosa 'Doris Taylor'
Echinops 'Green Gold'
Eriogonum sp.
Feijoa sellowiana
Francoa ramosa
Gaura lindheimeri
Iberis sempervirens

STRINGFELLOW GARDEN
Aeonium pseudotabuliforme
Agave americana
Artemisia 'Powis Castle'
Aster x frikartii
Bougainvillea spectabilis
Buchloe dactyloides
Cedrus deodara
Cerastium tomentosum
Ceratostigma plumbaginoides
Chamaemelum nobile
Dianella tasmanica
Echium fastuosum
Epidendrum ibaguense
E. x obrienianum
Erigeron karvinskianus
Erodium chamaedryoides
Euphorbia characias 'wulfenii'
E. x martinii
Geranium x incanum
Hibiscus rosa-sinensis
Iris x germanica 'Breakers'
Jacaranda mimosifolia
Juniperus chinensis
    'Robusta Green'

Laurus nobilis
Lavandula multifida
Leptospermum laevigatum
Nymphaea 'Tina'
Parthenocissus quinquefolia
Phlomis fruticosa
Phyllostachys nigra
Platanus racemosa
Punica granatum
Romneya coulteri
Rosa banksiae 'Alba Plena'
R. 'Belle of Portugal'
R. 'Mermaid'
Senecio mandraliscae
Strelitzia reginae
Thymus serpyllum

MARTIN GARDEN

Acacia cultriformis
A. glaucoptera
A. melanoxylon
A. redolens
Acanthus mollis
Aeonium arboreum 'Zwartkop'
Agapanthus africanus
Agave americana
A. americana 'variegata'
A. attenuata
A. desmettiana
A. parryi huachucensis
Aloe arborescens
A. bainesii
A. barbadensis
A. marlothii
A. speciosa
A. striata
A. thraskii
Alyogyne huegelii
Anigozanthos flavidus
Arctostaphylos 'Emerald Carpet'
A. densiflora 'Howard McMinn'
A. manzanita 'Dr. Hurd'
Artemisia 'Powis Castle'
Aster x frikartii
Baccharis pilularis 'Twin Peaks'
Bougainvillea 'California Gold'
Buchloe dactyloides '609'
Butia capitata
Carex sp. (Calif. native)
Ceanothus 'Concha'
C. griseus
    'Carmel Creeper'

Cerastium tomentosum
Ceratostigma plumbaginoides
Cereus
Cistus x hybridus
C. skanbergii
Convolvulus cneorum
C. mauritanicus
Corokia cotoneaster
Cotoneaster dammeri
    'Coral Beauty'
Cotyledon orbiculata
Crassula falcata
Cupressus sempervirens
Distictis buccinatoria
Dodonaea viscosa 'Purpurea'
Dorycnium hirsutum
Dracaena draco
Dudleya brittonii
D. hassei
D. pulverulenta
Echeveria 'Black Prince'
E. harmsii
E. x imbricata
Echium fastuosum
Eucalyptus globulus
E. torquata
Euphorbia characias 'wulfenii'
E. cotinifolia
E. x martinii
Fatsia japonica
Feijoa sellowiana
Geranium x incanum
Globularia x indubia
Hardenbergia violacea
Helichrysum petiolatum
    'Limelight'
Heteromeles arbutifolia
Iris x germanica 'Breakers'
Jacaranda mimosifolia
Juncus patens
J. polyanthemus
Kalanchoe beharensis
Kniphofia uvaria
Lavandula angustifolia
L. dentata
L. multifida
L. stoechas
Leptospermum laevigatum
L. laevigatum 'Reevesii'
Leucodendron 'Safari Sunset'
Melaleuca decussata
Melianthus major

Miscanthus transmorrisonensis
Muehlenbeckia axillaris
Muhlenbergia dumosa
M. rigens
Myoporum parvifolium
Nandina domestica
Nerium oleander
Nymphaea 'Tina'
Oenothera berlandieri
Olea europaea
Ophiopogon planiscapus
    'Nigrescens'
Opuntia Ficus-indica
Oscularia deltoides
Parthenocissus quinquefolia
Pelargonium tomentosum
Pennisetum caudatum
P. setaceum 'Rubrum'
P. 'Burgundy Giant'
Phlomis fruticosa
Phormium 'Jack Spratt'
P. 'Maori Chief'
P. tenax
P. tenax 'atropurpureum'
Pinus halapensis
Pittosporum undulatum
Protea neriifolia 'Pink Ice'
Puya laxa
Quercus agrifolia
Ribes sanguineum
Romneya coulteri
Rosmarinus officinalis
    'Lockwood de Forest'
R. officinalis 'prostrata'
Rychelytrum repens
Saccharum officinarum
    'Pele's Smoke'
Salvia 'Allen Chickering'
S. chamaedryoides
S. clevelandii
S. leucantha
Scaevola 'Blue Wonder'
Sedum 'Autumn Joy'
S. 'Red Carpet'
Senecio mandraliscae
S. reflexum
Stipa tenacissima
Strelitzia reginae
Tibouchina urvilleana
Westringia rosmariniformis
Yucca whipplei

Andree, Herb, and Noel Young. *Santa Barbara Architecture.* Santa Barbara, Calif.: Capra Press, 1980.

Angier, Belle Sumner. *The Garden Book of California.* San Francisco: Paul Elder and Co., 1906.

Belloli, Jay, ed. *Myron Hunt, 1868–1952: The Search for a Regional Architecture.* California Architecture and Architects Series, no. 4. Los Angeles: Hennessey & Ingalls, 1984.

Belloli, Jay, ed., et al. *Johnson, Kaufmann, and Coate: Partners in the California Style.* Santa Barbara, Calif.: Capra Press, 1992.

Bissell, Ervanna Bowen. *Glimpses of Santa Barbara and Montecito Gardens.* Santa Barbara, Calif.: Schauer Printing, 1926.

Byne, Arthur, and Mildred Stapley Byne. *Spanish Gardens and Patios.* Philadelphia: J. B. Lippincott Co., 1928.

Chandler, Philip E. *Reference Lists of Ornamental Plants for Southern California Gardens.* Los Angeles: Southern California Horticultural Society, 1993.

Church, Thomas D. et al. *Gardens Are for People.* New York: McGraw-Hill, 1983.

Cornell, Ralph D. *Conspicuous California Plants.* Pasadena, Calif.: San Pasqual Press, 1938.

Dobyns, Winifred Starr. *California Gardens.* New York: MacMillan, 1931.

Eckbo, Garrett. *Landscape for Living.* New York: Architectural Record with Duell, Sloan and Pearce, 1950.

Garnett, Porter. *Stately Homes of California.* Boston: Little, Brown, 1915.

Gebhard, David, and Robert Winter. *A Guide to Architecture in Los Angeles and Southern California.* Layton, Utah: Peregrine Smith, 1977.

Goldsmith, Margaret Olthof. *Designs for Outdoor Living.* New York: George W. Stewart, 1941.

Goodhue, Bertram Grosvenor. *The Architecture and the Gardens of the San Diego Exposition.* San Francisco: Paul Elder and Co., 1916.

Griswold, Mac, and Eleanor Welles. *The Golden Age of American Gardens: Proud Owners. Private Estates. 1890–1940.* New York: Harry N. Abrams, 1991.

Hanson, A. E. *An Arcadian Landscape: The California Gardens of A. E. Hanson, 1920–1932.* Edited by David Gebhard and Sheila Lynds. Los Angeles: Hennessey & Ingalls, 1985.

Hertrich, William. *The Huntington Botanical Gardens, 1905–1949.* San Marino, Calif.: Huntington Library, 1949.

Hockaday, Joan. *The Gardens of San Francisco.* Portland, Oreg.: Timber Press, 1988.

Jackson, Helen Hunt. *Ramona.* Boston: Roberts Brothers, 1884.

Keator, Glenn. *Native Perennials of California.* San Francisco: Chronicle Books, 1990.

Longstreth, Richard. *On the Edge of the World: Four Architects in San Francisco at the Turn of the Century.* Cambridge, Mass.: MIT Press, 1983.

Mathias, Mildred E., ed. *Color for the Landscape: Flowering Plants for Subtropical Climates.* Arcadia, Calif: California Arboretum Foundation, 1964.

———. *Flowering Plants in the Landscape.* Berkeley: University of California Press, 1982.

McLaren, John. *Gardening in California.* San Francisco: A. M. Robertson, 1908; 2d ed. 1927.

———. *Gardening in California: Landscape and Flower.* San Francisco: A. M. Robertson, 1909.

McWilliams, Carey. *Southern California Country: An Island on the Land.* Layton, Utah: Peregrine Smith, 1946; reprint 1983.

Mitchell, Stanley B. *Gardening in California.* New York: Doubleday Doran, 1936.

Moore, Charles et al. *The Poetics of Gardens.* Cambridge, Mass.: MIT Press, 1988.

Muller, Katherine K. et al. *Trees of Santa Barbara.* Santa Barbara, Calif.: Santa Barbara Botanic Garden, 1974.

Munz, Philip A. *A Flora of Southern California.* Berkeley: University of California Press, 1974.

Murmann, Eugene O. *California Gardens.* Los Angeles: Eugene O. Murmann, 1914.

Myrick, David F. *Montecito and Santa Barbara.* Vol. I: *From Farms to Estates.* Vol. II: *The Days of the Great Estates.* Glendale, Calif.: Trans-Anglo Books, 1988, 1991.

Newcomb, Rexford. *Old Mission Churches and Historic Houses of California.* London: J. B. Lippincott Co., 1925.

———. *The Spanish House for America.* Philadelphia: J. B. Lippincott Co., 1927.

———. *The Old Mission Churches and Historic Houses of California.* Philadelphia: J. B. Lippincott Co., 1925.

Padilla, Victoria. *Southern California Gardens: An Illustrated History.* Berkeley: University of California Press, 1961.

Peters, William F. "Lockwood de Forest, Landscape Architect, Santa Barbara, California, 1869–1949." Master of Landscape Architecture thesis, University of California, Berkeley, 1971.

Platt, Charles Adams. *Italian Gardens.* New York: Harper and Brothers, 1894.

Polyzoides, Stefanos, Roger Sherwood, James Tice, and Julius Shulman. *Courtyard in Los Angeles.* Berkeley: University of California Press, 1982.

Shepherd, John Chiene, and Geoffrey Alan Jellicoe. *Italian Gardens of the Renaissance.* New York: Scribner's, 1925; reprint, London: Tiranti, 1966.

Stanger, Frank M. *South from San Francisco.* San Mateo: San Mateo County Historical Association, 1963.

Starr, Kevin. *Americans and the California Dream, 1850–1915.* New York: Oxford University Press, 1973.

Streatfield, David C. *California Gardens: Creating a New Eden.* New York: Abbeville Press, 1994.

———. "The Evolution of the California Landscape." *Landscape Architecture* 130. Parts 1–4: "Settling into Arcadia" (January 1976), pp. 39–46; "Arcadia Compromised" (March 1976), pp. 117–26; "The Great Promotions" (May 1977), pp. 229–49; "Suburbia at the Zenith" (September 1977), pp. 417–24.

Weiskamp, Herbert. *Beautiful Homes and Gardens in California.* New York: Harry N. Abrams, 1964.

Wharton, Edith. *Italian Villas and their Gardens.* New York: Century, 1905.

Waters, George, and Nora Harlow. *The Pacific Horticulture Book of Western Gardening.* Boston: David R. Godine, 1991.

Yoch, James J. *Landscaping the American Dream: The Gardens and Film Sets of Florence Yoch— 1890–1972.* New York: Harry N. Abrams, 1989.